INDIA UNVEILED

Oh, East is East, and West is West, and never the twain shall meet,
Till Earth and Sky stand presently at God's great Judgment Seat;
But there is neither East nor West, border, nor breed, nor birth,
When two strong men stand face to face, though they come from the ends of the earth!

—Rudyard Kipling
The Ballad of East and West, 1889

Women admiring Jain sculpture. Adinatha temple. Ranakpur, Rajasthan.

INDIA UNVEILED

**Text and Photographs
by
Robert Arnett**

Atman Press

An early morning haze over the Hindu temples and the ruins of a 17th-century palace. Orchha, Madhya Pradesh.

India Unveiled
Text ©1996 by Robert Arnett
Photographs ©2006 by Robert Arnett
2104 Cherokee Avenue
Columbus, Georgia 31906-1402

Published by Atman Press
PMB #345, 2525 Auburn Avenue
Columbus, Georgia 31906-1376
(800) 563-4198
www.atmanpress.com

Publisher's Cataloging-in-Publication Data
Arnett, Robert, 1942-

India Unveiled
Text and Photographs by Robert Arnett

224 p. 31 cm.
115 lbs. gloss art paper
264 colored photographs
Includes glossary and index

ISBN 10: 0-9652900-4-2
ISBN 13: 978-0-9652900-4-3

Library of Congress Control Number: 2006925054

DS421.A76 2006
915.4-dc20

1. India—Description and travel. 2. India—Social life and customs. 3. Art—India. 4. Architecture—India.
5. Photography—India. 6. Religion and Culture—India.

Editor:	Smita Turakhia
Associate Editor:	Gail Greenblatt
Text Editor:	Ruchi Turakhia
Layout:	Smita Turakhia Robert Arnett
Maps:	Scott McIntyre
Designer:	Thom Hendrick

Printed and bound in Italy by Cover Communication S.r.l.
Via Lattanzio, 23 • 20137 Milano, Italy

Acknowledgements for photographs
All photographs are by Robert Arnett except those appearing on the following pages:

Ashok Dilwali, Kinsey Brothers, A-2 Connaught Place, New Delhi, India 110001. Pages 104-105.

Debasish Mukherjee, 91/U Joykissen Street, P.O. Uttarpara, Hooghly, West Bengal, India 712258. Page 106.

Shivji, Godavari Vallabh Niwas, Makarana Mohalla, Jodhpur, Rajasthan, India 342002. Page 85.

The Bhaktivedanta Book Trust International. ©1986, Faboret 101, S-242 97 Hoerby, Sweden. Photo used with
permission. Page 169.

Contents

An early morning fog in the Garhwal Himalayan Mountains near Badrinath. Chandrapuri, Uttaranchal.

Dedication

This book is dedicated to the memory of Paramahansa Yogananda, author of Autobiography of a Yogi, *and the other great masters of India. Through the ages, they have renounced all worldly possessions and dedicated their lives to bring to the followers of all faiths the sacred liberating science of yoga, by which the soul may be merged back into the One.*

Author's Notes

On a business trip to Detroit, Michigan in 1969, I met a young man at an exhibition of Far Eastern art. Our conversation turned to a discussion of Indian philosophy, about which I had very little knowledge. The exchange intrigued me, and as I would realize later, I was at a crossroad on my life's journey. My new acquaintance suggested that I read *Autobiography of a Yogi*. He then invited me to accompany him to a yoga service the following Sunday. My first meditation experience brought me to a level of consciousness which I had never known. That experience was the impetus which led to my in-depth study of Indian philosophy and the sacred science of Kriya Yoga, an ancient meditation technique whose devoted practice leads to direct, personal experience of God. The more I learned, the more I sought to know. I felt very strongly that I needed to return to a place I had never been, and in December 1988, destiny set my path towards India. Without itinerary or expectations, I began the first of three solitary journeys, each of which would last six months. It was during that short span of time on my second trip that my life was transformed. Not only was the Indian subcontinent unveiled to me, but in the process, I discovered the true essence of my being.

For thousands of years, the basic cornerstones of Indian culture have changed very little. As a result, historians acclaim India to be the oldest living civilization on earth. Modern excavations and scientific research reveal that Indic tradition has an unbroken cultural continuity that goes back at least 10,000 years. Archeology and other evidence support the position that there was no Aryan invasion. Vedic India is one of the oldest documented civilizations on earth, and through its religion, culture, and Sanskrit language, it has had a profound influence on Europe and much of the rest of the world. Based on the new corpus of knowledge, it is time for the West to revise the factual inaccuracies in its depiction of the origin of civilization. There is no justification to perpetuate an outdated account of history formulated during colonialism, which ignored India's formidable cultural antecedents.

This book is a tribute to the traditional values of modern India, which were already mature in the 5,000-year-old Indus-Sarasvati civilization. One of these concepts is *Vasudhaiva Kutumbakam*, humankind as one family. Another is the concept that God is One, even though the paths that lead to Him are many. A third is the principle of *dharma*, or righteous action, which is expected from all people under all conditions. Today, in our divisive world, Vedic India's wisdom becomes increasingly more important if our multicultural society is to share our planet in peace.

Modern India, like the rest of the world, is in a state of major transition as her people grapple with the enormous task required to balance science and modern technology with the inner peace of the soul. Although Indian culture has had the resiliency to withstand over 300 years of Mughal conquest, I wondered if it could survive the effects of Western materialism on its growing middle-class. I now know that my concerns were unfounded. My travels throughout India revealed that Hindu values are deeply ingrained in its society. Not only will India be able to assimilate Western technology into its own culture, but it will be stronger for it. Long after the modern buildings in cosmopolitan Mumbai (Bombay) have been reduced to rubble by time and the elements, the eternal verities of village India will be as vibrant as ever.

Robert A. Arnett

Foreword

By Roy C. Craven Jr.
Professor of Indian Art History, Emeritus
University of Florida, Gainesville
Author of *A Concise History of Indian Art*, Thames and Hudson, London

Ever since Alexander the Great came out of the mountain passes of Afghanistan onto the plains of North India in 326 B.C., Westerners have been reacting and recording their impressions of the rich, multi-hued culture of India.

The narrative which follows is a remarkable accounting of one American's rigorous pilgrimage across India to confirm his spirituality and to search out India's reality. This intense journey takes Robert Arnett from Gujarat and the sands of the Thar desert in the west—to Calcutta and Bhubaneswar in the east—to the extreme southern tip of the subcontinent at Rameswaram and Kanyakumari—to the icy visions of the high Himalayas seen from Darjeeling and Kashmir—and, along the way, to the numerous ancient and remarkable sacred sites, of the genre only to be found in India.

Robert Arnett's journey is defined by his explorations for the sacred in great modern cities and in small villages as well as in the remote shrines and ashrams of gurus and swamis. This is achieved by traveling nights and days on trains and crowded country buses.

Through it all the traveler has preserved for the reader a complex collage of scenes, sounds, and personalities which coalesce into a mosaic of Indian land and personalities—and along the way the pilgrim and his quest are revealed as well.

This is a narrative of feeling and devotion which will move the reader by its rich scope and emotion.

View of the snow-capped Himalayan mountain range as seen from Darjeeling, West Bengal.

A view of a bathing ghat at late morning. Varanasi (Banaras), Uttar Pradesh.

A man drying a recently dyed cloth. He is standing on a rocky bluff overlooking the Narmada River. Omkareshwar, Madhya Pradesh.

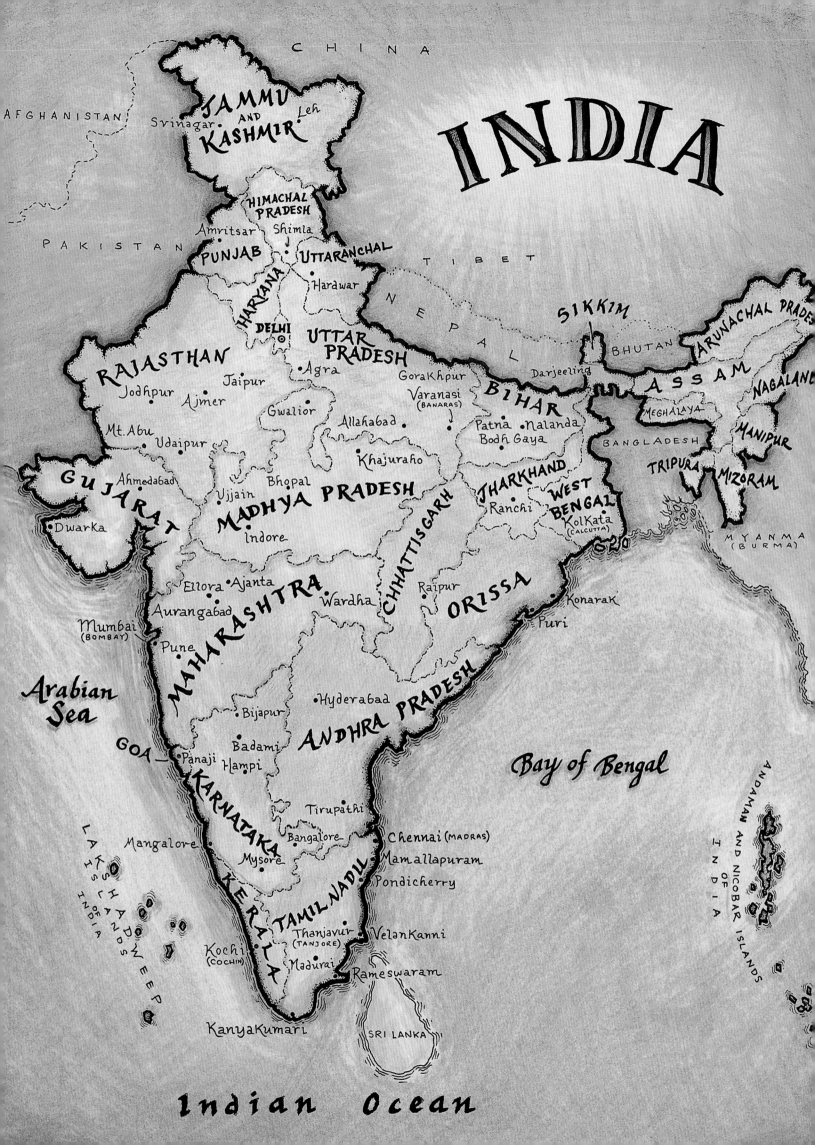

Introduction

India is one of the oldest river-valley civilizations in the world and is one of the few countries whose original culture, language, and religious beliefs still exist. The term "Indian" applies equally to a Hindu, Muslim, Christian, Sikh, Jain, Buddhist, Parsi, Jew, or anyone who is a citizen of India. The word "Hindu" refers only to a follower of Hinduism, the name given to a collection of the ancient scriptures of India, the Vedas, whose four books are known as India's *Sanatana Dharma*, Eternal Religion. The name "Hindu" came from the Greeks, who invaded northwestern India under Alexander the Great. They designated the inhabitants on the banks of the Indus River as Indoos, or Hindus.

Over the years, India has witnessed the rise and fall of many empires and invasions by people of various races and cultures. The Muslims began invading northern India as early as A.D. 1000. Their political domination ultimately fell to the British who ruled India for most of the 19th and first half of the 20th centuries, until India's independence in 1947.

With over one billion inhabitants who live in a space about one-third the size of the United States, India is now the world's largest democracy. It has the second largest population in the world, ranking behind China. India is still overwhelmingly rural, and its economy is predominantly agricultural. Although it has over 20 cities with a population of more than a million, about 70 percent of the population still live in rural areas. In the villages, life is unhurried, and only changing seasons mark the passing of time.

According to some historians, at the time India was conquered by Western colonial powers, it was one of the wealthiest nations in the world. References to India's riches are also found in the Bible and in ancient Greek, Roman, and Chinese literature and prompted Christopher Columbus to look for a shorter European trade route to India, leading to his discovery of the Americas. India's wealth was so great that she became the "Jewel in the Crown" of the British Empire, but the systematic transference of India's resources during foreign domination completely upset its economic structure.

There is still widespread poverty, but with an affluent middle class that is larger than the population of the United States, India is now one of the largest markets for consumer goods in the world. In addition to being a major industrial and nuclear power, India is a world leader in information technology.

Cultural Diversity

More than any other nation in the world, the diversity of India's religions accounts for much of its cultural richness. It has been home to the cultural heritage of people from almost every religion and philosophy, who have lived together harmoniously for thousands of years. Innumerable monuments, exquisitely carved temples, stupas, mosques, churches, forts, and palaces dot the country's landscape. Its ancient heritage intertwines with modern development and has given India its unique identity.

Even within India's state boundaries, there are a myriad of ethnological differences, which include religions, languages, customs, celebrations, and foods. Because of such a diverse population, India has been referred to as a continent within a country.

Languages

National homogeneity is virtually unknown, which is not surprising in a country with no "Indian" language. The constitution recognizes 18 languages. It is difficult for a Westerner to comprehend how a country can have over 1,650 languages that are considered mother tongues! Most of the languages have their own script. Even trying to decipher Indian body language could be perplexing. In parts of India, if someone shook his head horizontally from side to side, the mannerism meant "yes."

Introduction

Though Hindi has been designated India's official national language, it is the primary tongue of less than a third of its people. Hindi is spoken predominantly in the North and has little similarity to the Dravidian languages of the South. Opposition to Hindi in the South is not unexpected, and naturally, each region prefers to use its own language.

The absence of a common Indian language partially accounts for the fact that English, introduced into India by the British, is still widely used, even though India received its independence from the British in 1947. In national politics, English is the most important language, and many top officials still address their colleagues in English. English also is the language of commercial communications. I noticed tour guides often routinely spoke English in addressing Indians from other regions. My finding someone who spoke English was seldom a problem, although there were times on local country buses when no one knew the language, and I had to fend for myself. Even when sign language failed, I never missed my stop.

The school systems in most states in India teach three languages: English, Hindi, and the vernacular of that particular state or region. In addition, some students learn the ancient Sanskrit, which is the classical literary language of the Indian scriptures and also is the world's oldest surviving language. Western linguists concur that Sanskrit (which consists of fifty letters, each one having a fixed, invariable pronunciation that prevents mispronunciations) is the most perfect phonetic language in the world. George Bernard Shaw agreed. He wrote a wise and witty essay urging the adoption of a new English alphabet with 16 additional characters, which would approximate the phonetic perfection of Sanskrit, even if "it cost a civil war!" Because of Sanskrit's pleasing sound and meter, I usually could distinguish it from Hindi or the local dialects. Often, hearing prayers chanted in Sanskrit would evoke a tingling sensation within me, as if it was resonating in my inner core.

Religion

India is the birthplace of four major religions: Hinduism, Buddhism, Jainism, and Sikhism, and is an important home to Zoroastrianism, one of the world's oldest surviving religions. Hindus make up about 80 percent of the population of India. Muslims are India's largest minority and account for about 12 percent of the nation. Jews have lived there for over 2,900 years, having come with King Solomon's merchant fleets. The earliest Christian community, the Syrian Orthodox, was established by A.D. 190, though according to a legend, the Apostle St. Thomas had arrived there much earlier.

Hinduism, India's majority religion, is greatly misunderstood in the West. Most occidentals do not realize that Hinduism is a monotheistic religion, in which God is beyond time, space, and physical form. The entire pantheon of gods and goddesses are symbolic representations of God's numerous qualities and His intelligence functioning in every aspect of creation. The One Unmanifested Supreme God is called Brahman (not to be confused with Brahma, the first part of the Hindu Trinity, or with *brahmin*, a Hindu priest). One of the Hindu scriptures, the Rig Veda, clearly states: "Though men call it by many names, it is really One."

Hinduism created a different deity for each of God's numerous qualities to make God seem more real and approachable. I noticed in the villages, many women preferred to worship Lord Krishna in the form of a baby rather than as a man, probably because it made it easier for them to share their maternal feelings for the Lord.

The earliest scriptures of Hinduism are the Vedas. These texts were passed down orally and were only transcribed during the last millennium. The corpus of the religion's sacred writings also include the ancient allegories the *Ramayana* and the *Mahabharata,* the world's longest epic poems. Their complex symbolism represents the physical, mental, and spiritual battles each of us must fight and win in our daily lives. Contained within the *Mahabharata* is the Bhagavad Gita, Song of the Spirit, the most beloved and sacred scripture of India. Its verses recount the sublime wisdom given by Lord Krishna to his disciple, Prince Arjuna.

It is difficult to define the religion. Hinduism contains various approaches to achieve its ultimate goal, oneness with God, and it can take a lifetime of study just to master even one of its many aspects. It has been said that every metaphysical thought that ever was, is, or ever will be—has already been expressed in Hinduism.

Hinduism embraces the doctrine of reincarnation, which declares that our unfulfilled material desires force us to return again and again to earth until we consciously attain oneness with God. Even the early Christian

Church accepted the principle of reincarnation, although this doctrine was declared a heresy in A.D. 553 by the Second Council of Constantinople.

Hinduism is a very tolerant religion. It does not claim exclusivity of the true God only for itself. Hinduism acknowledges that God took many human embodiments on earth, including saviors of other religions. A Divine incarnation is called an *avatar*, one who has attained union with Spirit and then returns to earth to help humankind. He is Divinity who has descended into flesh. Hindus consider Christ to be an *avatar*, but believe God also took form in other saviors such as Krishna and the Buddha. A Hindu sage and poet wrote, "I know Thou hast delighted, and wilt ever delight, in revealing Thyself in different forms...but Thou hast only one Nature: Perennial Joy."[1] Hindus also recognize the Divine inspiration of prophets such as Moses and Mohammed.

India has the largest Muslim population anywhere in the world outside of Indonesia. Muslims believe that the Qur'an, the sacred scripture of Islam, contains revelations that were given directly to the Prophet Mohammed by Allah (God). Islam shares common origins with Judaism, including the belief that creation began with Adam and that Ibrahim (Abraham) is an important prophet. The religion also recognizes as prophets Nuh (Noah), Musa (Moses), and Isa (Jesus). One of the pillars of Islam is that Muslims should make a pilgrimage to Mekkah (Mecca), known as *hajj*, once in their lifetime.

Sikhs number a little over 1 percent of India's population. Traditionally, they do not cut their hair, smoke tobacco, or drink alcohol. The men are easily recognizable by the distinctive style of their turbans and thick, full beards. Sikhism was founded in 1469 by Guru Nanak.

Descriptions of Buddhism, Jainism, and Zoroastrianism will be discussed in their respective chapters.

Like the United States, India is a constitutionally secular country with separation of church and state. India celebrates as national holidays the main observances of most major religions of the world.

Devotion

What impressed me most about India was the peaceful demeanor of her people and their openly expressed devotion. The following incident will illustrate both characteristics: after a four-hour bus journey from Chennai (Madras) to the South Indian town of Tirupathi, our guide informed us that we would not be able to continue our trip to the nearby holy mountain of Tirumala, as a local labor strike prevented our going further. Because Tirumala is one of the more important pilgrimage centers in all of India, the passengers were very disappointed, yet no one complained. Most were tranquil as we sat together in a group waiting to see what would transpire. We realized that missing our visit to the magnificent statue of Sri Balaji, the deity to whom the temple was dedicated, would be a great loss to us all. Hindus believe that prayer requests made standing before this statue will be granted, which explains why an average of 30,000 pilgrims visit there on any given day.

I struck up a conversation with one of the passengers who saw the labor strike as a man-made adversity that could serve as a spiritual challenge for all of us. His insight inspired me, and I joined the others in praying silently that our pilgrimage to Tirumala would somehow be completed. At that moment, such peace came over me that I had no doubt God would grant our request. Shortly after lunch, we were told that the strike had been canceled and the buses would transport us to the mountaintop. Through God's grace, I had been able to tap into the collective devotion of the pilgrims and to feel their all-pervasive love, which I believe changed the course of events. I learned a great lesson that day: prayer is more powerful than protest!

In a similar situation in other countries, most people would have complained vehemently. But not these pilgrims. Because of the value and historical proof in Indian life that prayer has worked for millenniums, there was no discussion. It was a given that prayer was the natural and proper course of action. More than in any other culture I know, Hindus have connected God with their daily life.

The deep devotion of Hindus to God, especially amongst women, seemed to me to be inborn. At most temples, when the services were over, a priest carried a flaming oil lamp among the worshipers. The flame symbolized that God is Light, and most persons present would pass their hands above the sacred lamp and touch their forehead in reverence for God's presence. The women in the temple usually rushed forward to receive the sacrament with such childlike enthusiasm that it was as if God was actually there.

I remembered the comments of a Hindu doctor whom I had visited in western India. He told me that "because of the devotional nature of the Hindu people, the foremost thoughts of the mother and the father are of God. This devotion manifests itself within the mother's womb during pregnancy through the influences of the parents' conscious and subconscious thoughts, and when the child is born, devotion is part of its nature."

Devotion expressed itself outwardly in various ways, including the strong sense of responsibility that individuals exhibited for their parents and members of their extended family. A man I met while traveling told me a poignant story. His mother had been in a coma in a Mumbai (Bombay) hospital. Against all hospital regulations, the man's wife insisted on staying in the same room and even slept on the floor to be close to her mother-in-law, ensuring that she was timely bathed and kept in clean clothing. Doctors and even the husband's relatives told her that the mother would not survive. But against all odds, she did! The mother had a total recovery and now lives happily again with her son and daughter-in-law. He commented, "Loving feelings can save a life."

The deep loyalty that exists between husbands and wives and other family members serves as a living example from one generation to another. An Indian doctor whom I had met told me that his father, a man of modest means, had paid his college expenses. The doctor, who had a large practice, said, "I am a doctor and a man today because of what my father sacrificed for me. If my father ever needed me, I would close my practice, withdraw my children from school, even if it meant their missing important exams, and take my family the several hundred miles to my father's home to care for him. I would not allow a servant to touch my father in my presence." To bathe and otherwise assist his father was the doctor's pleasure and duty. His children would see him serve his father, and in turn they would serve their father, and their children would serve them. The elderly die peacefully in India, surrounded by their devoted families, and in the familiar setting of their own homes. They have a soft death and pass on fulfilled. To me, this is the quiet beauty of India.

After having visited with many Indian families over a period of years, I am impressed by the sincerity with which each family member accepts his or her familial responsibilities. Duties were not discharged from a sense of obligation as if they were burdensome. An Indian I met on a bus explained: "Duty is performed from love and affection, like a mother taking care of her child." He said his mother and wife still serve in that spirit. Though there was some inconvenience caused from three generations living together in his home, he stated that his wife did not feel burdened by a house full of people and seemed to thrive on her selfless duties. He was emphatic that "action must be supported by feeling. Once it becomes a duty performed mechanically without feeling, the tradition ends!"

I do not suggest that Indians or any peoples of third world countries should deny themselves the material benefits of Western civilization, yet it seems to me that many young Indians (as well as the youth in much of the rest of the world) are forgetting the true values of the family structure. The attributes of duty, loyalty, and service are often forsaken in favor of selfish considerations and monetary gain. Many are moving away from their ancestral homes, opting to live even in the slums of cities, or moving to other countries, in search of treasures without value.

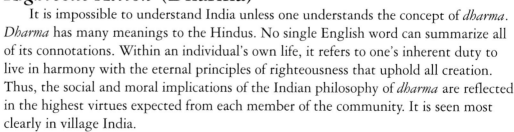

Righteous Action (Dharma)

It is impossible to understand India unless one understands the concept of *dharma*. *Dharma* has many meanings to the Hindus. No single English word can summarize all of its connotations. Within an individual's own life, it refers to one's inherent duty to live in harmony with the eternal principles of righteousness that uphold all creation. Thus, the social and moral implications of the Indian philosophy of *dharma* are reflected in the highest virtues expected from each member of the community. It is seen most clearly in village India.

I recall once in a small town in Rajasthan, a young boy saw me drop my wallet which contained a huge sum of money by his standard. When he came up to me to return it, I tried to offer him a few rupees, but he would accept nothing. I asked someone nearby to explain to the boy why I wanted to give him something for his act of honesty. After talking to him, the man explained to me that the concept of accepting a gift for doing a good deed made no sense to the child. *Dharma* is a noble act and needed no outside reward.

The Guest Is God

Though I come from an area of the United States where people pride themselves on their Southern hospitality, it could not compare to the gracious treatment I received in India. I was treated so thoughtfully in all the homes I visited, whether rich or poor. On several occasions, in modest homes, my hosts insisted on sleeping on the floor so that I could use their bed. I was not allowed to do even the most simple chores, such as helping to clear the table after meals. Even when my departure from a home was extremely early in the morning, the hostess always insisted on preparing breakfast for me and made sure the children were awake and dressed to say goodbye.

Non-Attachment

I learned quickly to limit my compliments for any objects I saw in an Indian home, as my hosts offered me almost anything I admired. The willingness of the Indians to give away their prized belongings prompted me to examine the value system of my own country, where the need to acquire more and more stuff is a major goal of life. In the Bhagavad Gita, Lord Krishna emphasizes the importance of non-attachment to the things of the physical world. If one does not carefully distinguish between the soul and the ego, then one's physical and spiritual focus is directed outward toward the object of temporary values. In the end, all worldly things return to dust, but the soul can return to God.

India's Gift to the World

India's spiritual heritage is legendary. Throughout the millenniums, India has been blessed with more masters—persons who during their lives on earth have merged their souls with God—than any other country in the world. There are many well-documented stories of their miracles. The famous master Trailanga Swami, who lived in Varanasi (Banaras) during the late 19th century, weighed over 300 pounds though he seldom ate. He displayed miraculous powers that cannot be dismissed as myth. Until recently, there were living witnesses to his amazing feats. Many persons witnessed him drink the most deadly poisons with no ill effect. Thousands of people saw him levitating in a sitting position on the surface of the Ganges River for days at a time. He would even disappear under the waves for long periods, and reappear unharmed. The yogi never wore any clothing and, on several occasions, was arrested and locked in a cell by the police for his nudity. Each time, even with posted guards, he unexplainably escaped with his cell still locked. The police had no clue as to how he did it.

For over 2,300 years, travelers from the most powerful countries on earth have come to India in search of her priceless spiritual wisdom. When Alexander the Great returned to Persia after his unsuccessful invasion of India, the most valued treasure he brought back with him was not gold, jewels, silk, or spices—but his guru (spiritual teacher), the yogi Kalyana, called Kalanos by the Greeks.

On a designated day in Susa, Persia, the sage Kalanos gave up his aged body by entering a funeral pyre in view of the entire Macedonian army. The soldiers were amazed that the yogi had no fear of pain or death and never once moved from his position while being consumed by flames. Kalanos embraced many of his close companions before leaving for his cremation, but refrained from bidding farewell to Alexander. To him Kalanos simply remarked: "I shall see you later in Babylon." Alexander died a year later in Babylon. The Indian guru's prophecy was his way of saying that he would be with Alexander both in life and death.

When the Chinese traveler Hiuen Tsang attended a huge religious gathering, the *Kumbha Mela*, in Allahabad in A.D. 544, he recounted that Harsha, king of northern India, gave away the entire wealth of his royal treasury to monks and pilgrims attending the event. When Hiuen Tsang prepared to return to China, he declined Harsha's offerings of jewels and gold. Understanding that his spiritual development was more valuable than worldly wealth, he accepted instead 657 religious manuscripts. Likewise, through the science of yoga, India has given the West a far more valuable gift than all the material wealth or technology the West could give in return. Even today, India offers great inspiration to those persons who are seeking oneness with God, and through yoga anyone can find the direction one needs to succeed. That is India's gift to the world.

Large sculptures of Jain Tirthankaras (saints) carved into the cliffs on the approaches to Gwalior Fort. Gwalior, Madhya Pradesh. Mid-1400s. Restored.

Chapter One

Central India

◁ *Opposite*
Vishvanath
Temple,
Khajuraho.
Chandella
dynasty, ca.
A.D. 1002.

Madhya Pradesh and Chhattisgarh

India comprises 28 separate states and seven territories. Madhya Pradesh is the geographical heartland of the country. Much of this state is located on a high plateau, and like most of India, it can be uncomfortably hot and dry in summer. Most Western travelers only visit this part of India to see the famous temples at Khajuraho, known for their erotic carvings. But the state does have several other towns that are among my favorites in all of India.

The great Buddhist masterpiece at Sanchi, with its rich iconography of elephants, solar discs, and scenes from the Buddha's life, should not be missed. Omkareshwar, the pure and unspoiled sacred Hindu island replete with humble village pilgrims and boats with upturned bows, is also well worth a visit. Both of these magnificent sites are remote but can easily be reached by local buses. Located about 30 miles south of Bhopal, the capital of Madhya Pradesh, is Bhimbetka, known for its numerous rock paintings.

The state of Chhattisgarh was created from Madhya Pradesh in the year 2000. Its new capital is Raipur. The division occured because political scientists as well as political activists had long argued that India's larger states were too big and needed to be broken into smaller regions for better administration.

Opposite ▷
*People entering a medieval
temple. Khajuraho. Chandella
dynasty, ca. A.D. 950–1050.*

*Javari Temple silhouetted
at sunset. Khajuraho.
Chandella dynasty,
ca. A.D. 1075–1100.*

Khajuraho

Khajuraho's splendid temples, which draw travelers from all over the world, are one of India's most frequently visited attractions. Originally, there were 85 ornate Hindu temples, but only 22 remain. Most of the medieval temples that still stand date from A.D. 950 to 1050, which partially accounts for the site's architectural cohesiveness. In addition, the Vishnu and Shiva sects of Hinduism, as well as Jains who built there, all employed the same style.

My bus arrived late in the evening, and after checking into a hotel, I went in search of food. Though Khajuraho is a small town, it has a wide variety of places to eat. Because it was a pleasant night, I chose to dine at an outdoor restaurant lighted only by candles. I ordered an all-you-can-eat vegetarian *thali*, which meant I would be served as much of the four vegetable preparations as I desired. The inexpensive meal was excellent and was one of the best values that I had in all of India. Any of the single servings would have been worth the cost of the entire meal. I had requested that the proprietor use less spicy seasonings than he normally would, and to my delight, the meal was prepared perfectly to my taste. All the dishes were delicious, including the fried okra, which made me a little homesick for southern American foods. Though *dhal* (lentils) is included in all basic fare, the thick sauce gave this staple legume a gourmet flair. I always enjoyed mixing yogurt with the *dhal*, and used a *chapati* (thin, flat bread) to scoop it up. Although silverware was provided, using one's fingers is the accepted way to eat in most places in India. The owner evidently knew how to cook for Westerners. The *palak panir* (spinach with cubed, soft cheese) was not overcooked. A delicate combination of coriander and cumin turned what appeared to be the thinly sliced stalk of a very plain vegetable into a tasty curry, which I ate with *basmati* rice. The meal was so good that it took willpower not to overeat.

Khajuraho is famous for its erotic sculptures. No one seems to be sure why the erotic figures were carved. The most carnal sculptures of Khajuraho probably represented the sexual excesses of a philosophy called Tantra. These Tantric practices were eventually cast out by the alienated worshipers and priests of Hinduism who considered them taboo.

The shikhara *(tower) of Kandariya Mahadeo Temple rises to a height of 102 feet. Khajuraho. Chandella dynasty, ca. A.D. 1025–1050.*

The *shikhara* (tower) of the great Kandariya Mahadeo Temple rises to a height of 102 feet and dominates the entire landscape. Hundreds of figures are carved in vertical bands that seem to be a natural part of the buttresses which support the tower. It is a perfect integration of art and architecture. The clever design of the giant tower directed my gaze upwards as successive levels culminated at the top. Its effect was as if heaven and earth had merged, which was the purpose for the tower being built directly over the most sacred part of the structure. The inner sanctum, or "holy of holies," enshrines an image of Shiva, the deity to whom the temple is dedicated.

Each temple is impressively situated on a high stone platform. Because of the additional elevation, I had to raise my eyes upwards to view the entire structure, which made it seem even more grandiose.

Although today's traveler sees these soaring towers in their weathered sandstone color, during the Medieval period when the temples were built, they were coated with white stucco to create the illusion of being snow-covered peaks of the Himalayan mountains. Even without the white coating, I stood in awe of these graceful structures.

Sculptural detail. Jain. Parsvanath Temple. Carvings from this temple are considered to be among the finest at Khajuraho. In the center, a heavenly nymph is applying eye make-up. Chandella dynasty, ca. A.D. 950–970.

A heavenly nymph removing a thorn from her foot. Vishvanath Temple. Khajuraho. Chandella dynasty, ca. A.D. 1002.

A heavenly nymph holding a mirror while applying a mark (bindi or tilik) at her spiritual eye. Mahadeva Temple. Khajuraho. Chandella dynasty, early 11th century.

After spending the morning photographing, I rented a bicycle to visit some other temples located about a mile away. Shortly after leaving the bicycle shop, I saw a young girl of about eight walking by the side of the road, probably returning from school since she was carrying her book bag. She was wearing a sweater and skirt whose length covered her knees. A piece of fancy white lace sewn near the hem made the homemade garment seem special. When she approached a roadside Hindu shrine that had a bell suspended beyond her reach, she climbed upon a concrete post so that she could ring it.

While a bell has an esoteric meaning in most religions of the world, a Hindu rings one upon entering a temple or shrine to attract the attention of God, much the same way as we ring a doorbell to let someone know that we are there. This little girl was spontaneously trying to get God's attention to express her devotion. Her gaze of concentration as she rang the bell indicated that she had serious business with the Lord. In a way, she was talking to Him, saying, "Lord, here I am. Don't forget me."

I jumped off my bicycle and captured the event on film. Her sincere devotional outpouring of love for God touched my heart. While most travelers to Khajuraho remember it for the erotic stone carvings, my fondest memory is of this young girl ringing the bell by the roadside shrine.

A girl ringing a bell at a Hindu roadside shrine to attract God's attention. Khajuraho.

◁ *Opposite*
A priest performing a Hatha Yoga posture in front of a statue of Hanuman, dating to A.D. 922. Hanuman Temple. Khajuraho.

A Hindu priest standing in the Betwa River after his daily bath. Orchha, Madhya Pradesh.

Sunrise silhouettes palaces built during Orchha's golden age. 17th century.

Orchha

One of the least visited but most picturesque places in all of India is Orchha. Today, it is just a quiet village, but in the 17th century it was the capital of a powerful kingdom of the Rajputs, a group of warrior clans who controlled the northern state of Rajasthan. Their golden age included a palace built in Orchha for the Mughal emperor Jahangir. Many of the town's splendid palaces have survived the centuries in excellent condition, and because so few tourists visit the isolated area, it was as if I had somehow stepped back into that colorful era myself. Being able to stay in one of the few rooms at the Hotel Sheesh Mahal, located in a wing of the Jahangir palace, was an additional delight. It surely must be the most romantic place to stay in Madhya Pradesh.

I will always remember the view from my room after waking up early one morning and going to the window to open the shutters. The mist rising from the meandering river cast a haze over the rural countryside. Spired Hindu temples, surrounded by patches of verdant grasses, and ruins of a small palace looked more like a scene from the chateau country of France than Central India. For the briefest moment I thought that I must be dreaming. I grabbed my camera and rushed to the rooftop to capture this ethereal scene (see photograph after title page). Considering the well-preserved palaces, the regal simplicity of my hotel, and the savory Indian cuisine, I could not have asked for a more pleasant stay than my idyll in Orchha.

A painting depicting mounted Rajput warriors. Lakshmi Narayan Temple. Orchha. 19th century.

Sunset as seen from the palace roof. Orchha.

Royal tombs (chhatris) on the bank of the Betwa River were memorials to Orchha's rulers. Orchha. 17th–18th century.

Rock shelters. Bhimbetka.

A hunting scene. Bhimbetka.

A procession. Bhimbetka.

Painting depicting man's relationship to nature. Bhimbetka.

Bhimbetka

Bhimbetka has some of the earliest works of visual art created on the Indian subcontinent. On craggy cliffs dramatically rising from the surrounding landscape, some 1,000 cave and rock paintings have been discovered.

Painted with natural red, white, and terracotta cream pigments, the paintings are remarkably well-preserved. The academic consensus is that the oldest paintings date to at least 5500 B.C., though some scholars believe they could be over 30,000 years old. Regardless of their age, the simple geometric style of many of the paintings offers a visual testimonial to India's cultural continuity, which can be seen today in the Warli folk art of peoples who live in Madhya Pradesh and in the adjacent states of Gujarat and Rajasthan.

Bhopal

Bhopal, the capital of Madhya Pradesh, was built on the site of a 11th century city founded by the legendary Raja Bhoj. The present city was laid out by an Afghan chief who administered the city under Aurangzeb's reign, and at the emperor's death in 1707, carved out his own small kingdom.

Today, Bhopal is known for the Union Carbide disaster, in which poisonous gas escaped from a plant in December 1984. The deadly chemical cloud killed over 4,000 people in the world's worst industrial disaster. The real story of the city is its Mughal history, which dates back to 1707. As my bus came over a hill and approached the outskirts of the city, one of India's largest mosques dominated the view.

Eager to get a closer look, I immediately went to the mosque and entered its walled courtyard through a massive main gate. The three imposing white domes over the main structure were reflected in a square pool of azure water located in the middle of the courtyard. The two minarets flanking the front of the building were so tall that I had to crane my neck to see their tops.

Small groups of students were sitting around in the courtyard. Older men were teaching them from the Qur'an. I could feel such strong undercurrents of peace as I stood there that it gave me hope that someday there will be harmony among all religions. I walked over to one of the scholars to learn some additional history about the mosque, and we began a friendly discourse. He said to me very proudly, "We are making a big investment in our future. We are teaching our youth to be human beings." Evidently they were succeeding, for several of the teenage Muslim boys who came over to meet me were models of politeness.

Muslim students studying the Qur'an. Taj-ul-Masjid (mosque). Bhopal.

An estimated 10,000 worshipers bow facing Mekkah (Mecca) during a holiday, Eid-ul-Fitr, celebrating the conclusion of Ramadan. Taj-ul-Masjid (mosque). Bhopal.

Several years later, I had the good fortune to attend the holiday celebrating the end of Ramadan at that same mosque. During Ramadan, Muslims observe a month-long daily fast from dawn until sunset.

The courtyard was jammed with worshipers. I was the only Westerner there and possibly the only non-Muslim out of perhaps 10,000 worshipers. I noticed that all the men were wearing the traditional round Muslim cap, a *kufi*. I went to the mosque's office and asked if I should cover my head or wear a cap. The administrator broke into a big smile as he replied, "Just pray with your head uncovered." I thought to myself, he understands the true spirit of religion. Though I was unfamiliar with the Muslim ritual of how and when to bow, no one seemed to mind. Afterwards, several Muslims greeted me cordially, and I was glad I had participated in the prayers.

Muslims praying at conclusion of Ramadan. Taj-ul-Masjid (mosque). Bhopal.

A yakshi, female tree spirit. East Gate. Sanchi.

Sanchi

I was eager to get to the famous Buddhist site at Sanchi. While looking out of the window on the bus during the short journey from Bhopal, I saw an old man digging with a pickax by the side of the road. As he labored, he also attended a baby sleeping peacefully in a rope cradle that was tied between a fence and a telephone pole. As our bus continued towards Sanchi, we passed a large group of village women who were swinging heavy pickaxes and transporting broken stones in large containers skillfully balanced on their heads. They were dressed in colorful saris and wore an abundance of silver jewelry. I was surprised at how finely the women were dressed and how they managed to keep themselves so clean while doing their menial jobs. At one of the local stops, a young peasant woman boarded with four children. Their cheerfulness while standing in the crowded aisle during the entire journey was amazing. The oldest girl, about 10 years old, often held her baby sister, to give her mother a rest. She cradled her so lovingly that the baby was as content with her sister as she was in her mother's arms.

On a hill rising from the wide plain of Central India stand some of the oldest Buddhist structures in that country. Architecturally and artistically, Sanchi is India's most impressive Buddhist site. It is the four magnificently carved gates, 34 feet high, that make the site famous. Depicted on the square columns of the gates and their elegant, triple cross-members are episodes from the life of the Buddha and his previous incarnations.

The dome of the Great Stupa (shrine) was embellished with an outer covering of bricklike stone added at the end of the 1st century B.C. It is believed to be the first use of stone masonry on a building in India.

The Great Stupa (shrine) of Sanchi, as viewed from the north. Shunga and early Andhra dynasties, 3rd century B.C.—early 1st century A.D.

Inner face of western gate (torana) *at Sanchi. Scenes from the life of the Buddha, winged lions, the* stupa, *and the wheel. Andhra dynasty, late 1st century B.C.–early 1st century A.D. Sandstone.*

The shape of the simple domed *stupa* dates back more than 2,200 years; its architectural origins stem from primitive stone-covered earthen burial mounds. As Buddhism spread throughout Asia, the *stupa's* simple shape evolved into different forms: the pagodas of Burma and China, the *chorten* of Tibet, and the "world mountain" of Borobudur in Central Java, considered by art historians to be the greatest of all Buddhist *stupas*.

The Great Stupa of Sanchi does not directly connect to the events of the Buddha's life. It did not become an important religious center until approximately 200 years after it was built by the great Mauryan emperor Ashoka, who made Buddhism the official state religion in 255 B.C. He began a vigorous building project in Sanchi which continued for almost 1,000 years, though most of the ancient buildings are in ruins today.

With the gradual decline of Buddhism after the 7th century A.D., the hill was slowly abandoned and eventually forgotten, as it was covered by dense vegetation until its discovery in 1818 by a British officer.

It was after dark when my bus arrived in Sanchi. Early the next morning, I walked to the top of the hill where the famous *stupa* is located, overlooking the green plains below. For Buddhists, the ascent to the summit merely begins their pilgrimage. Immediately upon passing through the famous gates to the sacred site, the supplicants are drawn into a prescribed circular pathway to be followed in a clockwise direction. Depending on their devotion, they prayerfully circumnavigate the *stupa* three, seven, or for the most pious, 108 times. In earlier days, the pilgrims climbed stairs onto the roof of the shrine, a symbol of the Buddha's transcendental state of *nirvana*. Bolstered by the knowledge that a relic of the great sage is contained in the structure beneath them, the devotees strive to achieve sacred harmony with the higher world. Because of my love for religious art and architecture, standing in front of the Great Stupa was like being a pilgrim myself.

Ujjain

After so many bus trips, the comfort of traveling by train was a joy. The camaraderie within the compartment of a coach often becomes an event itself. Having sufficient food to eat was never a problem. Indian travelers frequently pack picnic meals that they often shared with me. Express trains offered inexpensive hot meals, or I could buy food from the vendors who passed up and down the aisles. At major stations, the platforms were filled with small stands and rolling carts which sold a variety of foods, fruits, vegetables, and drinks. Someone within my compartment usually spoke English, and by the end of the trip, we often exchanged addresses.

The ancient city of Ujjain is located on the right bank of the Shipra River and has numerous temples situated along its banks. Ujjain is one of the four sacred cities that host a huge religious festival drawing millions of pilgrims. The event, the *Kumbha Mela*, which lasts about a month and takes place every three years, rotates consecutively among Allahabad that is located 85 miles west of Varanasi (Banaras), Nasik about 115 miles northeast of Mumbai (Bombay), Ujjain that is 420 miles southwest of Agra, and Hardwar located 138 miles northeast of Delhi on the Ganges River in the Himalayan foothills. These sites were chosen by fate as gods and demons quarreled in heaven over an elixir which promised immortality to the one who would drink it. As they fought, a drop fell on each of these four fortunate cities.

In India, devotion is often expressed and represented by flowers. Usually a worshiper would not go to a temple without taking an offering. I selected a pink lotus for my flower offering at the Mahakaleshwar Temple. The lotus is an ancient symbol in India because its unfolding petals represent the expansion of the soul. Its purity and loveliness blossoms from the mud of its origin, forecasting a spiritual transformation for all.

Young girls holding prasad (*divinely blessed sweets*) *which they received inside a Hindu temple. Ujjain.*

A Jyotirlinga, *representing God's presence in the universe. Mahakaleshwar Temple. Ujjain.*

Religious students who have come to Ujjain to study at Mahakaleshwar Temple, home to one of India's twelve sacred Shiva shrines known as a Jyotirlinga. Ujjain, Madhya Pradesh.

Indore

The 50-mile bus trip from Ujjain to Indore took almost two hours. I was going to visit a friend I had met in Ahmedabad, where we were both guests in the same home. When I arrived, my host's wife prepared warm water for me on a gas burner so I could take a hot bath. My host, who was about 50, was an attorney and used a room of his two-story home as an office. They had two children, a son who was studying for his high school diploma exams and a daughter who was 15 years old. I had mailed them a postcard saying that I was coming, and they had been waiting for me since that afternoon. Their son Bunti addressed me as Uncle, and I grew to like the appellation and its significance.

That night, my host told me about a pilgrimage he and his wife had made to Jammu in the Himalayan Mountains of northwestern India. The elevation was approximately 18,000 feet and required considerable physical exertion, since it was a several days' climb completely by foot. His facial expression softened as he reminisced about how peaceful it was meditating there on the banks of a glacier-fed river. His wife confided that she had felt so satisfied inwardly in that spiritual environment that she thought seriously of not returning—a remarkable statement for a woman who was totally dedicated to serving her family. A physical malady made it difficult for her to walk, and just making the trip required tremendous determination and devotion. Accounts such as these increased my admiration for the Indian tradition to seek God.

Lord Shiva, King of Yogis, seated in the lotus position, garlanded with marigolds. The mosaic decoration of the shrine is made from small pieces of colored glass. Hindu temple, Indore.

◁ *Opposite
Shrine figure underneath a banyan tree on the bank of the Shipra River. Painted stone and flowers. Ujjain.*

Women selling flowers on the steps leading to the famous Sri Omkar Mandhata Shiva temple. Omkareshwar, Madhya Pradesh.

The holy island of Omkareshwar. Home to one of India's 12 most sacred Shiva temples, it is also the location where Shankara, India's most illustrious philosopher, met his guru.

Omkareshwar

Omkareshwar is built on the banks of the sacred river Narmada. Two of India's 12 great Shiva temples were said to have been located on the island in the middle of the river. My purpose in going there was to pay homage to the memory of one of the wisest minds the world has ever known. His name was Shankara. The thought of walking in his footprints thrilled me.

It is believed that Shankara was born in a small village of Western Malabar in southern India. Though the date of his birth is uncertain, many scholars assign him to the 8th or early 9th century. By the age of 10, he was an academic prodigy, having read and memorized all the Hindu scriptures. He also had written commentaries on many of them, and famous scholars from all parts of the country came to seek his scriptural interpretations.

Shankara's father died when he was a young boy. He persuaded his mother to allow him to renounce the world, and he took the monastic vows of poverty, chastity, and obedience.

It was on the banks of the Narmada River at Omkareshwar that Shankara met the famous philosopher and seer, Gaudapada, who had attained oneness with the Divine. The young boy asked the old man to initiate him, but instead, he sent the lad to his foremost disciple, Govinda Jati, who accepted him as his disciple and instructed him in meditation and the entire process of yoga. In a surprisingly short time, Shankara achieved complete Self-realization, the union of soul with Spirit.

Boat ferrying pilgrims across the Narmada River. Omkareshwar.

A shrine. Offering coconuts represent the surrendering of one's ego. Sri Omkar Mandhata Temple. Omkareshwar, Madhya Pradesh.

During Shankara's lifetime, India was passing through a period of spiritual decadence. Hinduism was on the wane, having been encumbered by priestly dogma. Buddhism, too, was in a state of decline. Many Buddhists misunderstood what was required of them if they were to attain the transcendental state of *nirvana*. They thought that to reach the void of *nirvana* meant total annihilation of the self. But the Buddha was referring to the ego, the little self, which must be overcome before the higher Self, a soul entrapped in a physical body, can attain liberation. It was during this era of spiritual confusion that Shankara brought timely reform to Hinduism. Redefining the goal of life as being one with the ever-existing, ever-conscious, ever-new bliss of Spirit, he taught a positive interpretation of God that was very much needed in the world. Not surprisingly, many followers of Buddhism turned to his teachings, and millions came to listen to the practical wisdom of the barefoot young monk.

Shankara was a rare combination of a saint, scholar, and teacher. In his brief 32-year lifespan, he visited every part of India, spending many years in arduous travel. He established *maths*, monastic education centers, in the four corners of India to promote religious and national unity. These influential centers still exist and are located in Mysore in the South, Puri in the East, Dwarka in the West, and Badrinath in the Himalayan North.

Having mastered yoga, Shankara had developed extraordinary powers that many Westerners attribute only to Jesus. A mental feat credited to him concerned his disciple Sanandana, who wrote a commentary on the philosophy of the *Brahma Sutras*. The manuscript was destroyed by fire, but Shankara, who had only glanced through it once, repeated it word for word to the author. The text, known as the *Panchapadika*, is still studied.

When seated on a riverbank one day, Sanandana heard Shankara calling him from the opposite shore. As he faithfully entered the swirling current to go to his guru, his feet were supported by a series of lotus flowers which Shankara materialized on top of the water. Sanandana was thereafter known as Padmapada (lotus-foot). Even more spectacularly, after Shankara's beloved mother died, he cremated her body with heavenly fire that spurted forth from his upraised hands.

As the morning light began to burn away the mist that hovered about this ancient village, I thought of the power of clarity Shankara had given not only to the Indians of that time, but also to the many generations that followed. As I walked the well-worn path into the small town of Omkareshwar, I passed over a small hill from which I got my first look at the sacred island. I had no preconceived image of what Omkareshwar would look like, and I had not expected such an ethereal landscape. The large island consisted of a steep, rocky hill whose prominent landmark was the massive tower of a Shiva temple. The scene looked like a 17th-century classical painting by the French artist Nicolas Poussin. A haze blurred the scene, giving the appearance that the island rose from the river. This view could have been Poussin's sought-after fantasy.

It was as if I were standing in the painting's foreground on clearly definable soil. Separating me from this holy island was the blue-green water of a river perhaps 40 yards wide. On the other side was the longed-for paradise of Arcadia, which always seemed to be illusive and just over the next horizon.

My visit to Omkareshwar was one of the great unexpected pleasures of my trip to India. I had never heard of it until my host from Indore suggested that I go there. I felt that the invisible hand of destiny

An ascetic (sadhu) *holding a Shiva trident. Omkareshwar.*

was again guiding my life, and I was grateful to have made a pilgrimage to this pastoral location where Shankara had attained his enlightenment.

I returned to Indore in time for the evening meal. After dinner, my host recited a few Sanskrit prayers so I could hear the euphony of the language. He evidently made mistakes on several occasions, because his wife and daughter would laughingly correct him as if he were a schoolboy who had made an error in his recitation. Though they did it good-naturedly, at that moment his role as head of the family was unapparent as he meekly smiled in embarrassment. Later, when we were alone, my host confided to me that I meant a lot to him, and that if I ever needed to, I could come live with his family.

One evening, when he asked me how many sisters I had, I replied, "None." The word was scarcely out of my mouth when his daughter Gudia, with whom I had become quite close, emphatically said, "One!" Her reply reminded me of my visit with a family in Ahmedabad in the state of Gujarat. When I referred to myself as "Uncle," my host's daughter immediately said, "Brother." And when her brother said to me, "We think of you often," she blurted out, "Always!" Such spontaneous outpourings of love and devotion deeply touched my heart.

Gwalior

Gwalior is famous for its large old fort, built atop a hill that rises over 300 feet above the old town and dominates the surrounding countryside. During the fort's 1,000-year history, it changed hands many times, including twice to the British. As I walked up the long ascent, turrets topped by domed cupolas serving as ominous sentinels reminded me of the many invaders who must have paid with their lives trying to conquer it.

My trip to Gwalior made a lasting impression on me because of my visit to the tomb of a Muslim Sufi saint. I spotted the structure's large roof from the ramparts of the Gwalior Fort and was curious to see what the edifice might be. Upon arriving at the site, I was told that the saint was Mohammed Ghaus, who had lived during the

16th century. Though Hindus and Sufis share a common heritage springing from the Vedas, I was surprised to learn that Hindus and Muslims worshiped at the same shrine. Considering the long history of antagonism which has existed between followers of the two religions, this was remarkable.

Though turmoil often exists in India between different factions, her religious communities have lived together harmoniously in spite of selfish motives of some zealots. I witnessed Hindus and Muslims sharing the same shrine in Gwalior, Hindus and Buddhists worshiping at the same religious site in Darjeeling, and Hindus and Christians praying together at the Church of Our Lady of Good Health in Velankanni in South India. Even Guru Nanak, the founder of the Sikh religion, is revered not only by Sikhs, but also by Hindus and Muslims. Because of the tolerance of Hinduism, I believe that eventually India will become the example for global ecumenism, showing today's multicultural world that peace is possible amongst diverse populations.

My journeys to Omkareshwar, Sanchi, and the mosque in Bhopal were inspiring and the memories endearing. Though Omkareshwar is Hindu, the *stupa* at Sanchi is Buddhist, and Bhopal's Taj-ul-Masjid is Muslim—God's peaceful vibration makes no distinction for religious and cultural differences.

The tomb of Mohammed Ghaus, built in 1564. The Muslim Sufi saint is revered by the Muslims and Hindus, and they both worship there. Prayer requests are posted on the tomb. Gwalior.

The imposing Gwalior Fort dominates
the surrounding countryside. Gwalior,
Madhya Pradesh. 17th century.

Surya Temple. Konarak, Orissa. Eastern Ganga dynasty, ca. A.D. 1240.

Chapter Two

The East

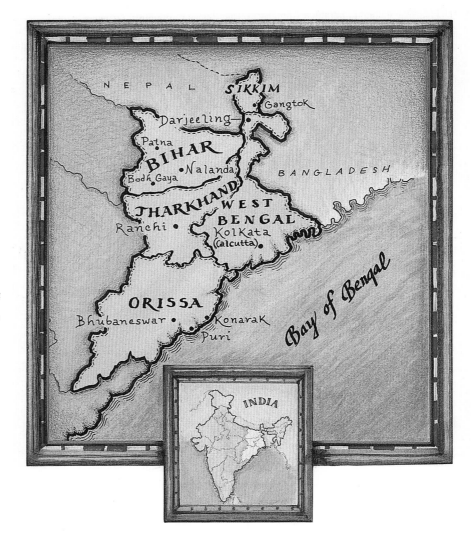

◁ Opposite

A statue of the Sun God Surya at the Surya Temple. Konarak, Orissa. Eastern Ganga dynasty, ca. A.D. 1240.

West Bengal, Sikkim, Orissa, Bihar, and Jharkhand

The scenery and cultural diversity of the four states included in this region are striking. Spectacular snow-topped Himalayan mountain ranges surround West Bengal's Darjeeling and the neighboring Indian state of Sikkim. Further south, the landscape quickly flattens into the basin of the Ganges River. Continuing eastward, the mighty Ganges flows onward to the coast, where its tributaries form countless estuaries, and its sacred water finally empties into the Bay of Bengal. About 35 miles from the coast, the sprawling city of Kolkata (Calcutta) is located on the east bank of the Hooghly River, a tributary of the Ganges.

Orissa, the state south of West Bengal on India's eastern seaboard, is tropical and has sandy beaches which stretch for miles. Conveniently located close to one another are the three important temple towns: Bhubaneswar with its hundreds of Orissan-style temples, many over 1,000 years old; Konarak, famous for its mighty Sun Temple; and Puri, home to one of India's most famous religious festivals known for its giant floats which require thousands of men to pull them.

To the west is the state of Bihar, where I traced the footsteps of the Buddha to Bodh Gaya, the place where he became enlightened while meditating under a banyan tree. The state of Jharkhand was created from southern Bihar in the year 2000.

Most of the mountainous northeastern area of India, located east of Sikkim, is home to various ethnic groups. Many of these areas are off-limits to foreigners to protect and preserve indigenous tribal cultures, so I shall not include that region in this book.

India Unveiled   43

Kolkata (Calcutta): The Pulse of Bengal

I took an overnight express train to Kolkata (Calcutta). When the train stopped at major stations, the piercing shouts of vendors and noisy passengers and well-wishers caused me to yearn for the peace of the countryside. As the train departed, the rhythmic clacking of the wheels on the rails was a welcomed and soothing sound. Watching scenes flash by outside the window added to the mesmerizing effect.

When my train arrived in Kolkata early the next morning, Howrah Station was already teeming with people. Over a million travelers, hawkers, and porters use this massive Victorian terminal each day.

I made my way through the crowds to the sidewalk, where I stood in a line to hire a metered taxi. For those in a hurry, an abundance of unmetered taxis are available, and drivers charge whatever the market will bear. Upon leaving the station, we immediately crossed over the Howrah Bridge. This 1,475-foot long cantilevered bridge spans the Hooghly without any pylons in the river and is the busiest bridge in the world. Looking through my taxi's window, I observed the pedestrians' faces, on which timeless adversity had etched its unmistakable lines.

Kolkata is a recent city by Indian standards, dating back over 300 years, and is one of the more densely populated cities in the world. The city is named after the Kali Temple[1] (Kalikata), which was anglicized to Calcutta. Because Bengal had a large mixed Hindu and Muslim population, the land was divided between India and Pakistan during partition at independence in 1947, resulting in a swell of Hindu refugees to Kolkata. Partition probably affected Kolkata more than it affected any other major Indian city.

The conflict between India and Pakistan in 1971 and the creation of Bangladesh led to another flood of refugees, worsening Kolkata's already overcrowded conditions. It is estimated that the city is home to six million refugees from famine and war.

I was glad when we arrived at the *ashram*, or monastery, where I would be staying. The *ashram* was located about 12 miles north of Kolkata and offered seclusion from contact with so many people. It was built on the bank of the Hooghly in the suburb of Dakshineswar. The driver blew his horn, and someone opened the gate for us to enter. Once inside, I heard sacred music coming from across the river, and I tingled with delight. The peacefulness of the *ashram* enabled me to put others' misfortunes out of my mind for a while.

The guest rooms and meals were basic. The mattress was so thin that I had to place some clothes between it and the hard, wooden bedframe just to be able to sleep. Although the bed had mosquito netting, I made the mistake of not using it and was awakened sometime after midnight as swarms of mosquitoes attacked me in a feeding frenzy. I arranged the mosquito netting around the bed as quickly as possible and finally went back to sleep.

I awoke early the next morning to the exotic sounds of birds. I associated their calls with the jungles of South America. Their strange warbling created a counterpoint to the drone of a nearby ferry's outboard motor. It was only 6 a.m., and Kolkata was already offering me an overture to the day's grand performance.

I spent the morning and early afternoon in the solitude of the *ashram* grounds. Its peaceful environment was the perfect prescription for a tattered traveler whose nerves had become frayed from a frenetic itinerary. I mentioned to one of the monks that an American friend had given me 500 dollars to distribute among the poor. He replied they would be happy to have 100 dollars for a leper colony that they served, and suggested that I give the rest to Mother Teresa's mission for the poor and homeless. I was touched by his unselfishness.

Early the following morning, I walked to the nearby Kali Temple, which was built in 1847. Kali Temple has become famous in recent years due to its connection with the God-illumined yogi and philosopher, Sri Ramakrishna, who preached the unity of all religions. Although the temple did not open until 6 a.m., many pilgrims were already there. The men and women formed separate lines and entered from opposite sides. I noticed that most of them were carrying flowers

Sunrise at St. Paul's Cathedral. Built in the mid-19th century, it is a reminder of British Calcutta (Kolkata).

◁ *Opposite*
Flower stalls located near the Kali Temple. They sell red hibiscuses, the color associated with Kali. Dakshineswar/Kolkata (Calcutta).

Women waiting to enter the Kalighat Temple. The red powder (sindoor) *where hair is parted indicates a woman is married. Women traditionally cover their heads with their saris before entering a temple. Kolkata (Calcutta).*

for an offering, many of which were deep red hibiscuses, the color associated with Kali. Like the others, I was eager to see the black stone statue of Kali, which was said to have taken a human form in honor of Sri Ramakrishna, who once served there as a priest.

The female figure of Kali represents God in the aspect of eternal Mother Nature. The black, four-armed deity is standing on the recumbent white form of Lord Shiva, who represents the Infinite from which all activities of Nature originate. Her four arms symbolize two beneficent and two destructive attributes of the essential duality inherent in all creation. Wearing a garland of skulls, Kali can be awesome in her destructive role, as she annihilates all things back into the One, only to create again. In her function as Goddess of Destruction, she holds a severed head. By making inferences through the intellect, many assume that her sword is used only for human destruction, but it is also a symbol of her eternal vigil as she keeps guard over creation's planetary rhythms and balances. The message is that one should not seek absolute values in the relative world of nature, which is both benign and ruthless. The riddle of good and evil has been challenging humankind's minds since the beginning of recorded history.

After lunch at the *ashram*, I went to the nearby town of Serampore to visit a meditation *mandir* (temple) built to honor Sri Yukteswar, a yogic master of the 19th century. With incomparable discerning wisdom, his book *The Holy Science* documents the essential unity of Hinduism and Christianity.

On the bus returning to the *ashram*, the conductor gently tapped me on my shoulder and indicated I should move. To my embarrassment, I had been standing on the women's side of the bus! That was the only area outside of South India where I encountered separate seating sections for men and women on public buses.

I believe that separating the sexes in certain situations engenders respect for women. Over 40 years ago, an Indian master said that coeducation in the West had been a great failure because it had failed to teach moral principles. Considering the moral degeneration that has subsequently transpired, I wonder what he would have said today!

About 50 miles from Kolkata is the famous Shiva temple of Tarakeswar. Because of the many spectacular healings which have taken place there, Hindus regard it with the same veneration that Catholics have for Lourdes in France. Because of its reputation, I was eager to go there. The two-hour trip to Tarakeswar required that I

A yogi with his head buried in the ground, demonstrating his mastery over control of the body's life force. Tarakeswar.

first get across the Ganges River. The ferry was an open boat perhaps 15 feet long. The outboard motor was so old that flowers had been placed on it in hopes that it would last another day. Due to the strong current of the Ganges, the navigator had to aim the overcrowded craft upstream from our destination. The fare was three cents.

Once on the other side, I took a bicycle rickshaw to the railroad station, where I boarded a local train. At each of the many stops, more and more pilgrims crowded aboard. I did not have to ask anyone to tell me when we arrived at Tarakeswar, because almost everyone departed at that stop. I followed the hundreds of pilgrims through narrow winding lanes. Like other pilgrimage centers I had visited in India, both sides of the street were lined with stalls selling icons and religious mementos. At lunchtime, I looked for a place where I could get something to eat. Though there were many stalls with large pots of hot food, I could not find a restaurant which met my standards for hygiene. I bought my lunch from a vendor on the street who sold tasty morsels of chick peas served on a washed leaf for a penny each.

On the way to the temple, I passed a yogi with his head buried in the ground. Evidently, he could control at will the flow of his breath and the functioning of his internal organs. While it seemed a strange way to demonstrate *pranayama*, the control of life force in the body, I was impressed with his accomplishment. When I returned a few hours later, the large number of coins in his offering plate indicated that poor Indian pilgrims were also appreciative.

Witnessing such a phenomenal event was astounding. Many Westerners even refuse to consider that it is possible to live without breathing. From my study of yoga, I understood exactly what I was seeing. The only thing I could not comprehend was why scientists have not investigated the yogic mastery of control over the breath. Combined with its accompanying transcendental mental states, I believe that the control of life force is one of the more important concepts ever conceived by the human mind.

When I entered the sacred Tarakeswar shrine, I saw that the altar consisted of only a round stone. Without a marked beginning or end, it was an appropriate symbol of the Infinite, and I bowed in reverence to it. I returned to Dakshineswar just in time for the 5 p.m. meditation at the *ashram*. It had been a most interesting day.

One evening, I was invited to chant with the young male employees of the *ashram* at a small temple overlooking the Hooghly. Because it could not hold everyone, I sat outside on the steps. Their devotion more than compensated for the cacophony of their loud, untrained voices.

The next day, while having my camera bag repaired in a little shop near the *ashram*, the artisan and I became instant friends. While I was talking to him, three adorable children approached me. The proprietor taught me a few Bengali words which enabled me to greet them, and between smiles and giggles, we enjoyed each other's company. After departing, the older of the two girls came back. She carefully removed a small bundle, which contained a large leaf, from her dress pocket. As she unwrapped it, I realized that inside were sweets which she had received from the priest at a temple across the street. Wanting to share her blessing with me, she pinched off a small piece of the cake and placed it in my hand. Although I was fasting that day, I ate the tidbit because it was *prasad*. The little girl looked at me, smiled, and went happily on her way. Such devotional unselfish acts are among my fondest memories of India.

The artisan from the luggage shop took me to a store to assist me in making a needed purchase. The proprietor wanted to order food for us, but my friend told him I was fasting. When the shopkeeper asked me why I starved the body, I replied that since he was a Hindu, he would understand that we live by *prana*, cosmic vibratory energy, and were not sustained merely by food ("Man shall not live by bread alone"—Matthew 4:4). I added, "Even though I am an American, I know that!" He laughed heartily in agreement. What a pleasure it was to be in a country whose people are the most metaphysically inclined in the world. Almost any Hindu commentary on its scriptures will impress the reader with its deep spiritual insight.

My Indian friend, Shyamal, invited me to have lunch with him that weekend. He, his wife, and their two children lived in a one-room home. Though they were very poor materially, his wife's inner radiance belied their condition. She prepared a nice meal for us outside on a gas burner. After lunch, my host took me to the home of one of his neighbors. While there, I admired some crafts. As we were preparing to leave, the young artist offered to give me a large porcelain vase, but I explained that I could not accept it as it would get broken. She then brought me a small bouquet of artificial roses. I told her that I would use them for my daily meditation in front of my travel altar. Leaving the room abruptly, she returned clutching a bottle of perfume in the palm of her hand. She sprayed the artificial flowers so they would smell good for God. I still use the flowers at home on my altar. Though their fragrance has long faded, the memory of her devotional gesture is perennially present.

Shyamal and I made plans to meet again at his shop several days later. Usually, when I had an engagement with an Indian, I specified that the appointed time was G.M.T., Greenwich Mean Time, and not I.S.T., Indian Stretchable Time. However, I suspected that our rendezvous would be on an I.S.T. basis.

When I arrived, the shop was closed, so I sat on a wall across the street. Two men were digging a hole in the dirt lane. As they sank deeper and deeper into the earth, I became aware of my friend's tardiness. Finally, he appeared.

I had planned my arrival in Kolkata to coincide with the Durga Festival, one of the popular Indian holidays. It is celebrated throughout all of India, although its name varies regionally. Durga, the consort of Lord Shiva, symbolizes the feminine form of creation.

In West Bengal, elaborate images of Durga are made and placed in shrines which are specially built for the occasion. Some of the more impressive edifices, which are constructed by placing tightly stretched canvas over bamboo scaffolding, appear to be large temples from a distance.

Women buying green coconuts. Its juice is a popular drink. Women with red powdered faces have been consecrated by a priest at the Kalighat Temple. Durga Festival. Kolkata (Calcutta).

At the end of the holiday, the images of Durga are ceremonially immersed into the sacred Hooghly River and the shrines are taken down. What I could not understand as an American was how someone could take months making an elaborate shrine object and then toss it in a river—whether the water be sacred or not. Upon reflection, I realized that it was a graphic example of a culture that places greater importance on the spiritual than it does on the physical realm.

On a subsequent trip to India, my friend Shyamal asked me to accompany him and his family to his mother's village, located less than 100 miles north of Kolkata, near the border of Bangladesh. Naturally, I was thrilled with the opportunity and immediately accepted.

Durga traditional iconography. Durga Festival, Bagh Bazaar. Kolkata (Calcutta).

◁ *Opposite*
A Durga image being immersed in the Hooghly River
at the conclusion of the Durga Festival. Kolkata (Calcutta).

Village of Salua, West Bengal

We left by train for Shyamal's village a few days later. When we arrived, he hired a bicycle rickshaw to take our luggage and his children to his mother's home, while he, his wife, and I walked. We stopped in the small town at a sweets shop, where I bought an assortment of delicious-looking cookies as a gift for his mother.

Before entering her home, Shyamal and his wife knelt respectfully at his mother's feet, which is the custom. When I did the same, she seemed pleased, and placed her hands upon my head as if blessing me. Though she did not speak English, I could see that she was a sweet and simple woman. She lived in a simple house like one might expect to see anywhere in the tropics. There was also a small, separate structure that served as a kitchen.

She insisted that I sleep in the main bedroom, but I refused, knowing that either she or her son and his wife would have to sleep on the floor of the other small bedroom. I found a storeroom attached to the front of the house and insisted I stay there. When they saw I was serious, the space was cleaned and prepared for me. They said if I would come for another visit, they would cut a window in the wall for my comfort. Sure enough, when I returned two years later, that and other major improvements, including a brick veneer, had been completed.

Though the house had electricity, there was no indoor plumbing. The small bathroom and toilet enclosures were located outside, where a hand pump provided water. Several members of her family lived nearby, and her smiling daughter-in-law helped prepare our meals.

Early the next morning while I was exercising outdoors, I noticed several young children watching me. It is possible that I was the first foreigner they had seen. Later that day, I met the next-door-neighbor's son. He was about eight years old and spoke some English, the only child who could. His young friends were eager to meet me, and together they acted as guides and showed me the village. When they learned of my religious interest, they took me to meet all the neighbors who had built small shrines outdoors for a special observance dedicated to the Goddess Lakshmi. I was impressed with the artistic merit of some of the shrines, which appeared to be constructed of papier-mâché over a wooden frame.

At every home we visited, the owners invited me in for something to eat and drink. None of the villagers possessed much by Western standards, but they graciously offered whatever they had. I am not sure who had a better time, the children or I. Everywhere we went, two of them would hold onto each of my hands, and others who were walking behind were eager to take their place. Some of the older children carried their younger siblings.

Ferryboats.
Salua.

To the children's delight, the Lakshmi festival entitles them to go around to all the homes, where they are given special treats to eat. Carrying bags much like American children on Halloween, they happily accept what they are given. I noticed that my host's mother included the special sweets I had brought to her with her offerings.

I called my head guide "Young Gopal," a name which Hindus use affectionately to refer to the deity Krishna when he was a young boy. When Young Gopal saw me using my Swiss army knife one morning, he was impressed with its many blades and gadgets and asked me to give it to him. When my host's mother learned what he had done, she told him that he should never ask for anything of this world. Upon completion of my visit to the village, I did leave the knife with my host to give to Young Gopal's father as a gift for his son when he was old enough to use it safely.

While combing my hair one day, Shyamal's mother asked me to comb the hair (symbolically) of the statue of Krishna located on her altar. I knew that in her own way, she was reminding me to keep God always in my mind and to dedicate all of my actions to the Divine. I heard her chanting one morning, and her son proudly informed me that his mother had memorized the 108 names for Krishna, and that was what she was singing. The number 108 has mystical significance to various religions. In a similar manner to Hinduism, Orthodox Judaism assigns God 108 attributes.

When Shyamal and I were walking outside one evening, I heard voices and music coming from the other side of the village. I asked Shyamal if we could go there, and he replied, "Of course." With the aid of a small flashlight, we headed in the direction of the music. About 15 villagers were crowded into a small house. A man beat the rhythm on an Indian drum with the palms of his hands. The lead female singer had a small pair of cymbals, and a few other women had simple percussion "instruments." Though none of the villagers spoke English, it was not important. They spoke the international language of devotion. I was grateful that I knew a chant in Bengali, because they asked me to sing for them. After the group finished chanting, a special meal was served to honor their spiritual teacher, and they asked us to join them.

The goal of traditional Hindu music is to stir the soul to attain union with God. While popular Western songs are usually inspired by sentiments or worldly experiences and are composed to arouse the emotions, classical Hindu music was composed to direct the consciousness inward, which is why chanting is often included as a part of meditation. The Sanskrit word for musician is *bhagavathar*, which means he who sings the praise of God. Sharing in a *kirtan* (musical gathering) was another of the unique experiences in my Indian travels, and I will always remember the devotion of the villagers.

A woman cutting vegetables on adz, held stationary by her foot. Salua.

A man selling a papaya, using a rock as a weight. Market. Salua.

Kolkata (Calcutta), West Bengal

The Victoria Memorial. Kolkata (Calcutta). Constructed 1906–21.

After returning to Kolkata, I moved to a hotel within the city for my remaining few days. Visiting that overcrowded urban area was quite a contrast to the peaceful life of rural West Bengal.

The noisy sprawling metropolis has considerable urban problems, but what I remember most is its tranquil nature. Underneath the clamor of the city's commotion is a calmness. Even on crowded buses, if one focuses inwardly, peace emanates from everywhere.

Bengalis are known for being very creative, and many of them are among India's leading poets and artists. Their sophisticated movie industry produces art films comparable to those made in the West.

While in Kolkata, I met the ex-Mr. India. The 58-year-old man was still in good physical shape and traveled all over India to judge national contests. He introduced himself as the ex-Mr. India and said, "I am a muscleman. I know how to build muscles. But now I want to learn how to build the mind." After devoting his entire life to physical culture, he had learned that developing the body without the mind was of little value.

One of Kolkata's most noteworthy monuments from the British Raj period, the Victoria Memorial, is located downtown. The white marble museum has a huge dome and is situated at the southern end of a large green expanse known as the Maidan, which is almost two miles long and over a half mile wide.

I was eager to see if Mother Teresa was in the city. I went to the headquarters of her religious order, the Missionaries of Charity. An Indian nun told me that she was leaving on an international speaking tour early the next morning, but would probably attend chapel services that evening.

When I arrived at 6:30 p.m. for evening prayers, the dimly lighted chapel was already filled with nuns. They were kneeling on the concrete floor, spines erect and hands folded in supplication. They wore simple white cotton saris with their order's blue trim along the edges. Their head coverings were made of the same material. Most of them were Indians. Mother Teresa was not among them.

About 45 minutes later, I felt a magnetic force go through my body. I wondered if Mother Teresa had arrived. Turning my head to the rear, I saw the frail, petite woman enter. Though diminutive in stature, she was a spiritual giant. Without saying a word, her vibrations uplifted the destitute and gave hope to the despondent. Those with receptive hearts who came within her presence had their lives changed. She was indeed a saint.

Jute workers unconcerned by the ominous monsoon sky. Mayapur.

The Monsoon

The hot Indian summer starts near the end of March, and by June everyone has had it with the heat. Suddenly the sky becomes gray, and big drops of long-awaited rain begin to fall. There is a refreshing smell as water hits the parched earth. One has to be there to appreciate it.

Eventually, the rain comes down in torrents so thick that you cannot even see your hand. People flock to the streets, adults wearing clothes and children not. To Indians, the rain is bliss, heaven-sent. Many men take their shirts off and enjoy the sensation of the rain striking their bare skin.

Getting drenched with a loved one is considered very romantic. A candlelight dinner would never do for Indians what getting wet in the monsoon does. It is joyful rejuvenation of both man and earth. If the monsoon is delayed or shortened, it causes anxiety and disaster. The land must get one year's worth of rain in four to five weeks. It can be 110 degrees, but when the thunderstorms start, the temperature abruptly drops to the 70s. Then the sun comes out for a few days before the storms begin again. The pattern repeats for the duration of the monsoon. Next comes a visual feast. Everything becomes green. Flowers bloom everywhere. Gradually the intensity and frequency of the rain diminishes and then stops. It is over for another year.

*Prayer flags, Bhutia Busty Monastery, Buddhist.
Darjeeling, West Bengal. 19th century. In background
is Mt. Kanchenjunga, world's third-tallest mountain.*

A terraced tea plantation, Himalayan Mountains. Darjeeling.

Darjeeling: Queen of the Hills

Darjeeling is a fascinating hill station, a term used by the British for their highland retreats which enabled them to escape from the scorching summer heat of the Indian plains. During my visit in March, when the nights were still quite cold, I slept under four thick blankets. It is a peaceful town with beautiful cloud-capped mountain scenery. Straddling a ridge at an altitude of 6,400 feet, Darjeeling is surrounded on all sides by tea plantations built on steeply terraced mountainsides. Most of the buildings are wooden, some are dilapidated, and in the town itself, structures are crowded together. The upper parts of the town are joined to the lower areas by interconnecting narrow streets and flights of steps.

During my springtime visit, the Himalayan mountains were continually covered by mist and fog, except for a few hours at sunrise and just before sunset, when nature suddenly lifted her veil as if by magic. During those times, the view of Mt. Kanchenjunga, the world's third-highest mountain whose summit reaches 28,200 feet, was majestic.

Darjeeling was formerly called Dorje Ling, Place of Thunderbolts. The British recognized its potential as a site for a hill station as well as its strategic importance in controlling a key pass leading into Nepal and Tibet. By the mid-19th century, the British annexed the region from the politically weakened Raja of Sikkim and established tea plantations, which today produce some of the world's "highest" quality tea. Today, Darjeeling has a diverse population of mountain people from all over the eastern Himalayas, including many Tibetan refugees who fled from China.

One of Darjeeling's most picturesque Buddhist monasteries, Bhutia Busty, is a short walk down the mountainside from the main square. I arrived at the monastery late one evening. Large prayer flags fluttered noisily in the mountain winds. The 120-year-old monastery's gold facade and deep red roof stood out against the stark white background of the snow-covered Mt. Kanchenjunga.

After the Chinese invasion, many high-ranking lamas came there as they fled Tibet, but today the monastery is staffed by younger monks, most of whom were in their late teens and early 20s. Because of my interest and understanding of Buddhism, I was invited to lunch and the afternoon meditation the following day.

Ghoom Buddhist Monastery. Darjeeling.

A young boy, six or seven years old, beat the different rhythms of the chants on a drum. During some of the more difficult rhythms, the monk leading the prayers placed his hand around the little boy's to help him play the proper sequence of beats. For the most difficult portions, the monk played the drum himself. Once, when the young boy rang the prayer bell at the wrong time, or more likely was playing with it out of restlessness, the monk gently took the bell from the child and placed it out of his reach. At the appropriate time, he gave the bell back to the little boy to ring. I was impressed by how well the young child beat the rhythms and how still he sat during the prayer period, which lasted over one-and-a-half hours.

After the prayer session was over, the monk, who was in his late 20s, asked me if I felt special energy from the chants. His question indicated to me that he had. From the amount of love and affection the monk gave to the child, I suspect that the young boy will elect to remain in the monastery when he must make that decision in his later teens. While I was traveling in the neighboring state of Sikkim, I met a young man who had attended a Buddhist residential monastery school from ages 12 to 17. Though he enjoyed the monastic life and had his mother's approval, he was told that he had not progressed enough to join the order.

As I lay in bed that cold March night in Darjeeling, I gazed out my window towards the stars above the mountaintop and thought of the young boy who beat the ritual drum and rang the prayer bell. I reflected on the long road that lay before him, the path of inner discipline that he must master, and the normal childhood experiences he must forsake. I wondered if he would be able to withstand worldly temptations, or even be asked to take monastic vows. I silently wished him well, then fell asleep.

Opposite ▷

A Buddhist monk blowing a ceremonial trumpet. Ghoom Monastery. Darjeeling. The deep sound of the trumpet represents God's creative presence in the universe. Most religions have a similar sacred word testifying to the Divine Presence: Aum *to* Hindus, Om *to* Buddhists, Amin *to* Muslims, *and* Amen *to the Egyptians, Greeks, Romans, Jews, and Christians.*

The following morning, I had a cup of hot Darjeeling tea with breakfast. To my surprise, it tasted exactly like it does at home when I make it with a Twinings tea bag. Later, I walked into the town center and browsed in an antique shop in search of old Tibetan statuary. Three young girls of Chinese extraction entered. They were dressed in school uniforms and probably attended the nearby Catholic school. They asked for money, and the shopkeeper, misunderstanding their purpose, told them to get out and quit begging. One replied to him in perfect English, but rudely, that the money was for the poor and she was not a beggar. I am sure such outspoken language would not have occurred in Hindu India, where respect for one's elders is taught from birth.

On a subsequent trip to India, I visited Darjeeling in early November. The weather was still warm, and Mt. Kanchenjunga appeared to be only an arm's length away. The holiday of Diwali was about to commence. Diwali is a festive celebration which dates back historically to the time when lamps were lighted to show Rama the way home after his period of exile. It symbolizes the triumph of good over evil.

In Darjeeling, it is the custom for a brother to honor his sister during Diwali, although in most of India, this tradition is observed on a different occasion. The practice has its roots in Hindu mythology when an evil supernatural being was trying to kill a woman's brother. She covered him with flowers to hide him, and this action saved his life. During Diwali, a sister fasts all day until her brother arrives. She then places a garland of flowers around his neck and pours a ring of oil around him on the floor. As the oil is lighted, he stands encircled in flames, which symbolizes his sister's "ever-burning" protection. It is a very sentimental holiday. If one has no brother or sister, that person tries to help and befriend someone as though he or she were a blood relative. I noticed several men proudly wearing their garlands in public.

A few days later, on the morning of Diwali, I went to the Observatory Hill, situated adjacent to Darjeeling's town square at the top of a ridge. The park must have been named by the British, for its name belies its sacred use. The hill is holy to the Hindus and Buddhists and has numerous shrines. Two of them are shared by members of both religions. A Buddhist priest sat on one side of the shrine and a Hindu on the other side. Hindu pilgrims went to the Hindu priest to be blessed and to make their devotional offerings, while Buddhists approached theirs. I observed some worshipers who went to both the Hindu and the Buddhist priests for their blessings.

◁ *Opposite*
A woman and child in front of Buddhist prayer flags. Note the marking of the spiritual eye on their foreheads. Diwali festival. Observatory Hill, Darjeeling.

Men wearing garlands. Festival of Diwali. Darjeeling.

Young monks in training. Rumtek Monastery. Near Gangtok, Sikkim.

Sikkim

I traveled around the state by bus, which enabled me to see the mountain scenery—and my first yaks, which the farmers raise as livestock. As the bus slowly ascended the high mountain passes, it seemed as if I were viewing the terraced landscapes and green valleys below from an airplane. From mountain altitudes of 28,000 feet, where peaks are capped in snow all year, the terrain tapers down to a dense rainforest that lies at sea level.

Little is known of Sikkim's early history. In 1640, it became an independent monarchy. Sikkim controlled a key pass between India and Tibet, which is one of the reasons the British made it a protectorate in 1861. Nepalis began migrating into Sikkim after 1870. Most of the Nepalis who came to Sikkim were Hindus, and today they comprise its largest ethnic group. The people of Sikkim voted to become a state of India in May 1975.

Pelling/Pemayangtse Monastery

By far the most beautiful views of the Himalayan Mountains that I had seen in all of India were from the small town of Pelling. Mt. Kanchenjunga and the other peaks provided a magnificent panorama at sunrise and sunset. Billowing clouds often obscured the view during the day, but at dusk, a soft red glow illuminated them as nature cloaked the mountains in her mystic mantle of peace.

Located about a mile from Pelling is one of Sikkim's oldest and most important monasteries. It was founded in 1705 and belongs to the Tantric Nyingmapa sect, established in the 8th century by the famous Indian teacher Padmasambhava. The monastery looks out on the snow-capped Himalayan range containing Mt. Kanchenjunga. Inside are impressive Tantric wall paintings and large Buddhist statuary.

I took a short walk to a small, peaceful mountaintop monastery, where the two resident monks lived a life of seclusion. When the monastery is shrouded in mist and clouds, it appears as if it is floating in heaven.

The Himalayan Mountains tower over Darjeeling. West Sikkim.

Orissa

The three temple towns of Puri, Bhubaneswar, and Konarak, with its great Sun Temple, are situated close to each other in the state of Orissa. Bhubaneswar is on the heavily-traveled Kolkata-Chennai (Calcutta-Madras) railway line. When I went to buy a ticket in Kolkata for this journey, they were sold out, and I had to go to a special office for foreigners. Fortunately, there is a national railway policy of holding back a percentage of tickets for non-Indians. Otherwise, traveling by train would have often been impossible, since the multitudes of Indians often reserve their tickets far in advance.

Bhubaneswar

Bhubaneswar has some excellent Orissan-style temples. Their ornately carved beehive towers curve gently inward as they reach the top. Local guides proudly claim that at one time the city had over 7,000 temples, of which hundreds still stand. Most of them date from the 8th to 13th centuries. The largest and most famous is Lingaraj, which dates from circa A.D. 1000.

A woman in early morning devotion outside an Orissan temple. Bhubaneswar.

A sadhu (*ascetic*).
Bhubaneswar, Orissa.

Children doing schoolwork in an outdoor class. Konarak.

Konarak

About 40 miles from Bhubaneswar is the Sun Temple at Konarak (see pages 40-1), dedicated to Surya, the sun god. This masterpiece of medieval Orissan architecture was constructed from 1238 to 1264 and was probably never completed. It is famous for the huge, intricate chariot wheels carved around the base of the temple. Their spokes serve as sundials whose shadows give the precise time. The temple was conceived as a gigantic representation of the sun god's chariot and is pulled by seven sculptured horses. Its sandstone pyramidal roof soars over 100 feet and is a landmark for sailors far out in the Bay of Bengal. Like the temples at Khajuraho, Surya Temple at Konarak is covered with erotic sculptures. Konarak also may have been a center for a Tantric cult.

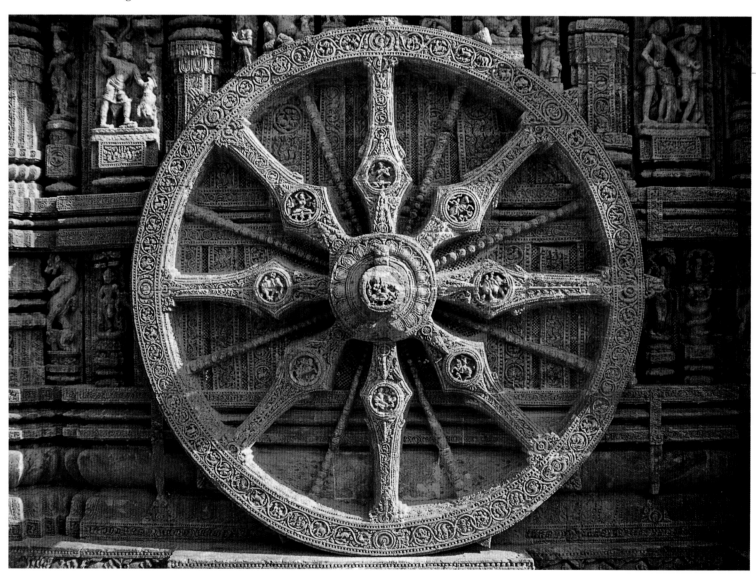

One of the 12 huge chariot wheels, almost ten feet in diameter, carved around the base of Surya Temple. Konarak. Eastern Ganga dynasty, ca. A.D. 1240.

Hindu ladies wading in the surf. Puri.

Puri

Twenty miles down the coast from Konarak is Puri, home of the Jagannath Temple. This seaside town is the site of one of India's greatest annual events, the Rath Yatra, which consists of huge "temple cars," or massive floats that require over 4,000 men to pull them down a broad avenue to a destination over a half mile away.

While I was in the ocean, I noticed that most of the younger women who waded into the surf were fully clothed. The women whom I recall most vividly were a group of four attractive college-age girls in their fine saris. It was refreshing to be in a culture where women do not blatantly use sex appeal to attract men, and virginity is still valued at marriage.

On my subsequent trips to India, the Western influence had made strong inroads into the culture of the youth. Indian movies and television shows now routinely included graphic scenes depicting female sensuality and partial nudity that would have been censored not long ago. I wondered if the sexual revolution and its overall negative effects on social values could be far behind. How quickly thousands of years of tradition are discarded.

The Bodhi Tree, the historical location of the Buddha's enlightenment and the most sacred Buddhist pilgrimage site in the world. Bodh Gaya.

Bodh Gaya

Bodh Gaya is easy to reach because the railroad junction at nearby Gaya is on the main Delhi-Kolkata (Calcutta) line. Even with a reservation, trying to board a train in overcrowded conditions is a hassle . On this day, I did not have a seat reservation for my train trip to Gaya. My first class, non-reserved ticket to Gaya entitled me to sit wherever I could—if I could. Since it was a day journey, I was not concerned. "Getting there" in India may not be half the fun, but it is half the experience.

When my train arrived, it had only one first-class car, and all of the seats were already occupied. A sympathetic group in another compartment saw me searching for a seat and motioned for me to come in. To make room for me and an English woman seeking a seat, an older Indian woman sat on the floor on a large rolled carpet she had purchased, and a younger lady squeezed in on the other side. A woman, two men, two teenage girls, and a child were now sitting in a space designed to comfortably seat three. We had all paid the same ticket fares, yet they packed together like sardines. Their thoughtfulness reinforced my respect for Hindu culture, and I hoped under similar circumstances Americans would be as courteous to foreigners.

The train arrived in Gaya shortly after 10 p.m. I walked across the street to the nearest hotel and ordered a bucket of hot water that arrived tepid. I then took an Indian-style bath by squatting and pouring water over my body with the small plastic cup which is provided along with a bucket in all bathrooms. By now I had become adept at pouring the water over my head and shoulders in such a skillful manner that the water would trickle down my entire body, wasting hardly a precious drop. After bathing, I went to bed.

The next morning, I was eager to make the eight-mile trip to Bodh Gaya where Prince Siddhartha (the Buddha's former name) became enlightened 25 centuries ago.

The large sacred Bodhi (banyan) tree shading the spot where Siddhartha gained enlightenment through meditation is not the original tree under which he meditated. A sapling from the original tree was taken to

A Buddhist pilgrim praying at the Bodhi Tree. Bodh Gaya. The trunk of the tree, at his left, is wrapped in colorful silk for a special ceremony. Gilded Buddhas in the background are recessed in the base of the Mahabodhi Temple.

A monk praying. Buddhist monastery. Bodh Gaya.

Sri Lanka by Emperor Ashoka's daughter when Ashoka brought Buddhism there. That tree still flourishes at Anuradhapura in Sri Lanka, and one of its saplings was brought back to Bodh Gaya.

Near the sacred spot is the Mahabodhi Temple, which was built in the 11th century. Its pyramidal spire rises over 150 feet and is similar to an earlier structure which was built on the same site. As I passed under the east gateway and through a long courtyard, the superstructure dominated the view. Equally impressive were the strong vibrations of peace which I could feel immediately.

The Buddha's Enlightenment at Bodh Gaya

The name "Buddha" means "The Enlightened One." He was born around 556 B.C. in a royal family in northern India, on the southern border of present-day Nepal.[2] The young Hindu prince's full name was Siddhartha Gautama of the Shakyas. Siddhartha, which means he who has achieved his goal, was his given name; Gautama was his surname; and Shakya was the name of his family's clan. When he became the Buddha at age 35, he was called Shakyamuni, sage of the Shakyas, symbolizing that he had attained an exalted state of consciousness by stilling his mind.

At Siddhartha's birth, the astrologers gave his father a disturbing prophecy about his son: he would become either a great emperor or, upon beholding the Four Signs (an old man; a sick man; a corpse; and a mendicant holy man, a *sadhu*), he would become an equally famous ascetic. Siddhartha's father was determined that his son must never see anything which might cause him to be dissatisfied with courtly life and restricted him to the palace compound. He made continuous efforts to keep the young prince's mind attached to the world and surrounded him with every conceivable luxury. At age 16, Siddhartha was married to a beautiful and devoted princess, who bore him a son.

Siddhartha grew into manhood thinking of the world as a place for endless happy events. But the prince was also curious about the world outside the palace grounds. One day, with his charioteer Channa, Siddhartha disobeyed his father's strict commands and secretly went to the nearby villages to see the world. On three successive outings, the handsome prince was shocked to the very depths of his being to see, for the first time in his life, a shriveled-looking old man, a dying man, and a corpse. He discovered that life was not as he had been taught to believe when he had been surrounded by his protective family within the walled confines of his luxurious palace.

On the fourth journey, after seeing a monk with shaven head and ochre robe, Siddhartha's desire for truth became so great that he decided to renounce forever his sheltered and luxurious life. One night, while everyone in the palace was asleep, he departed with a heavy heart on his "Great Going Forth" in search of truth which would give him complete understanding and mastery over the mystery of life and death.

For seven years, the prince practiced many austerities. Once, he grew so weak from lack of food that he fainted. This experience taught him that asceticism alone was not the way to enlightenment, but it was through the human body that man was to attain illumination. With this realization, Siddhartha gave up mortification and replaced it with the Middle Path. The body is given precisely the food and rest it needs for optimum functioning and nothing more.

The Buddha is credited with saying: "For the physical body of man lives only from day to day; if you supply it with what it actually needs, you will still have time to meditate, while if you seek to supply it with all it wants, the task is without end." The Buddha taught that by the Middle Path a wise person avoided both extremes of asceticism and self-indulgence as one follows a balanced life of calm detachment. He then began the final phase of his quest for enlightenment through concentrated thought and scientific meditation similar to the path of *Raja Yoga*.

One evening while meditating under a banyan tree, which is now known as the Bodhi Tree, or Tree of Wisdom, Siddhartha sensed that he was on the verge of enlightenment and vowed not to move until he obtained illumination. After remaining in meditation for 49 days and enduring many tests and hardships, salvation came. Declaring, "I will beat the drum of the Immortal in the darkness of the world," he arose from his seat under the Bodhi Tree and went to the Deer Park near Sarnath where he preached his first sermon to his former companions in austerities.

For the next 50 years, the Buddha traveled over much of the basin of the Ganges River. He shared with thousands his Middle Path to liberation or *nirvana*.

Mahabodhi Temple, Bodh Gaya. 11th century.

According to the Buddha, the principal cause of suffering is desire. He taught and accepted peasants and noblemen alike, regardless of their caste, and organized the original Buddhist orders of monks and nuns. His teachings include the Four Noble Truths, the Noble Eightfold Path, and the Wheel of the Law.

The Four Noble Truths are: 1. life is suffering; 2. the reason for suffering is desire; 3. suffering must be caused to cease by overcoming desire; 4. suffering will cease if one finds the path to deliverance, which is the Eightfold Path. The elements of the Eightfold Path are: 1. right knowledge or understanding; 2. right purpose or resolve; 3. right speech; 4. right conduct or action; 5. right occupation or a livelihood conducive to salvation, preferably the monastic life; 6. right effort; 7. right awareness or self-mastery; and 8. right meditation.

The Buddha used the Wheel of the Law allegory to illustrate the certainty of *karma*. Its symbol, the wheel, was a visual reminder of his teaching:

> That which ye sow, ye reap. See yonder fields!
> The sesamum was sesamum, the corn
> was corn. The silence and the Darkness knew!
> So is man's fate born.
> He cometh, reaper of the things he sowed.

The four most sacred sites connected with the life of the Buddha are Lumbini, his birthplace; Bodh Gaya, where he attained enlightenment; Sarnath, where he preached his first sermon; and Kushinagar, where he entered into *nirvana*.

A monk chanting in front of carved stone railing, Mahabodhi Temple. Bodh Gaya.

Prayer flags. The site of the Buddha's first sermon. Sarnath, Uttar Pradesh.

Reclining Buddha, signifying his entrance into nirvana. *Kushinagar, Uttar Pradesh. Gilded wood, silk.*

Buddhism is an offshoot of Hinduism, and rightly understood, the teachings are similar. Interestingly, Hinduism claims the Buddha to be the ninth incarnation of Vishnu, but perhaps it is just as well that Buddhism became a separate religion. By putting the purest Hindu wisdom into a simpler form, Buddhism has spread beyond India throughout Southeast Asia and has reached populations less keenly metaphysical, who might not have been receptive to the ancient Hindu faith.

Gaya

Just as Bodh Gaya is a principal pilgrimage site for Buddhists, nearby Gaya is a pilgrimage center for Hindus. Hindus traditionally go there to visit the Vishnupad Temple to honor their parents a year after their death. It is one of the most sacred sites to pray for one's ancestors. Twelve miles north of Gaya are the ancient Barabar Caves, which are the Marabar Caves of E. M. Forster's *A Passage to India*.

When I visited the Vishnupad Temple, I was looking forward to seeing the footprint of Vishnu that is said to be inside. Because of the large number of pilgrims, it was almost impossible to get to the statue of Vishnu. I offered my devotion at his footprint, which is imprinted on a solid rock and surrounded by a silver-plated basin. The footprint was covered with a clouded liquid that appeared to be a mixture of water, milk, and oil and had many flowers floating on its surface. I was told the 16-inch "footprint" could only be viewed at night. Since I was expecting to see Vishnu's real footprint, I stood there feeling embarrassed for being so gullible. I had a similar experience at a temple in Thailand, where I had keenly anticipated seeing a real footprint of the Buddha.

I was so inspired by the sanctity of Bodh Gaya that I decided to visit two other important Buddhist pilgrimage sites about 50 miles away.

Old seated Buddha. Bronze. Nalanda.

Rajgir and Nalanda

Early the next morning, I boarded a bus in Rajgir accompanied by a guide for the 12-mile trip to Nalanda, which was once a great center of Buddhist culture. It reached its peak of fame in the 5th century A.D. Leading scholars from China, Korea, Japan, Mongolia, Tibet, and Ceylon came there to study. The university once housed 10,000 students and was considered to offer the highest postgraduate education in Asia. The expenses for this monastic school were met by royal grants and endowments from the wealthy. The center flourished for 700 years until the monastery, university, and library were sacked and burned by Muslims in 1205.

I noticed a number of village women walking towards the nearby community. When I asked my guide where they were going, he replied that it was a special day. They were heading to the Sun Temple to make petitions to God. Many carried brass or copper containers filled with what appeared to be milk to be used as an offering. When I asked if we could visit the temple, he said, "Of course."

As we approached the temple, there was a steady line of petite, wet, shivering women streaming into the courtyard. They had bathed at a site perhaps a quarter of a mile away. On a freezing day when I had on my warmest clothing, they had on nothing more than thin wet cotton saris and shawls.

Inside, many of the women were making the traditional ritual circle around the interior of the temple, after which they poured the milky liquid from their vessels on a large, black stone sculpture of Vishnu. They stood silently as they offered their prayers to God. I was impressed by their devotion.

When we returned to Rajgir, my guide engaged a two-wheeled, horse-drawn cart to take us to a mountain made sacred by the presence of the Buddha. On the uphill grade, the driver used a whip to beat his horse on the underbelly. I could not stand the cruelty, so I asked my guide to tell him to stop and remind him that the Buddha had taught compassion for all beings, including animals. Still, he continued whipping the horse, who pulled as hard as he could.

I remembered a story of the Buddha passing through a village and seeing a lamb which was about to be sacrificed. He placed his own head on the chopping block and asked that he be killed instead. Touched by his compassion, many in the village became his disciples. With my guide as an interpreter, I asked the driver to whip me instead of the horse. When he later hit the horse again, I had my guide ask him if he would want himself as his owner if he were a horse. He stopped after that.

About halfway up the mountain, our cart had to pull off the narrow road to make way for a vehicle. As we stopped and waited, I became so engulfed in a wave of peace that I thought: "What is this?" As we pulled back onto the road to continue our journey, I noticed a small sign that said the Buddha often rested here on his way to the mountaintop. I was grateful for the circumstance which necessitated that we stop there.

We also visited the Bamboo Garden, where the Buddha lived for three years. Nearby is a Japanese monastery where a young monk beat a large drum every few seconds to awaken souls from the sleep of delusion. The rhythmic drumbeat shattered the silence and produced a haunting sound.

We walked to a hot sulphur spring crowded with people who took advantage of the unlimited source of heated water. It could be the only hot bath they would ever have. Behind it were steps leading up to a cave where it is believed that the First Buddhist Council met to write down the Buddha's teachings after his death. Before hiking up the mountain to the cave, I, too, enjoyed a bath in the hot mineral spring.

Regardless of one's religion, the principal sites connected with the life of the Buddha are worth visiting. They have a special peacefulness and sanctity about them.

Opposite▷
*Men and boys enjoying the
hot springs. Rajgir.*

Taj Mahal. Agra,
Uttar Pradesh. 1631–53.

Chapter Three

The North

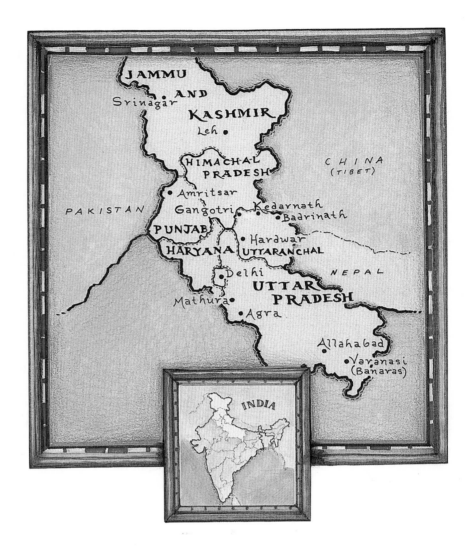

◁ *Opposite*
The Indus River near Leh,
Ladakh, in the state of
Jammu and Kashmir.

Delhi Union Territory, Uttar Pradesh, Uttaranchal, Himachal Pradesh, Jammu and Kashmir, Punjab, and Haryana

India's rich cultural diversity is most evident in the North. The Punjab is predominantly Sikh, Jammu and Kashmir has a large Muslim population, and the remaining states are overwhelmingly Hindu. A multicultural society presents India—and, indeed, the world—with the challenge of proving that large populations of different faiths can live harmoniously under one government. India is a great social experiment, and its outcome will influence the fate of the world.

Uttar Pradesh is one of India's more populous states. It is one of the states stretching across northern India in what is called the Hindi belt, where Hindi is the predominant language. Most of Uttar Pradesh is a vast plain. As the Ganges, India's most sacred river, flows across the plains towards the Bay of Bengal, it passes through Allahabad, one of the four cities which hosts a huge religious festival, the *Kumbha Mela*. Eighty-five miles east of Allahabad is Varanasi (Banaras), the holiest city to the Hindus. Nearby is the Buddhist pilgrimage site of Sarnath, where the Buddha preached his first sermon.

The mountainous state of Uttaranchal was created from northwestern Uttar Pradesh in 2000. It includes the Himalayan mountain range and the glacial source of the Ganges River. The important pilgrimage towns of Rishikesh and Hardwar are built upon the banks of the Ganges River in the foothills of that state.

A view of Shimla, a popular hill station. Himachal Pradesh.

A village woman in traditional clothing of that region. Naggar, Himachal Pradesh.

Much of the state of Himachal Pradesh is covered by the Himalayan Mountains. Located in picturesque settings are several cities which are well-known in the West. Shimla was the British summer capital. Dharamsala is now the Dalai Lama's home in exile from Tibet. Both are hill stations built on steep mountains. The beautiful Kulu Valley, with snow-capped Himalayan peaks forming its background, is called the "Valley of the Gods."

India's northernmost state has a double name, Jammu and Kashmir. Jammu is in the south. Its geography is a transition from the plains of India to the Himalayas. Further north is the Vale of Kashmir, a large Himalayan valley where the people are predominantly Muslim. Located in the remote northeastern part of the state is a high plateau known as Ladakh. In stark contrast to Kashmir and the rest of India, its culture is primarily Buddhist and Tibetan

The majority of India's Sikhs live in the Punjab. Located on India's northwestern border with Pakistan, Punjab was partitioned at Independence. The population included large numbers of Muslims, Sikhs, and Hindus. The region was divided into the Muslim state of Punjab, which became part of Pakistan, and a Sikh and Hindu Punjab that remained part of India. Horrible atrocities took place in 1948 as millions of Sikhs and Hindus migrated eastward and millions of Muslims fled westward to the newly formed Pakistan. In 1966, the Indian Punjab was divided again, creating the largely Hindi-speaking state of Haryana and the predominantly Sikh, Punjabi-speaking state of Punjab.

Old and New Delhi

Today's Old Delhi, as the name indicates, is built upon old cities and mixed traditions. Archaeologists have excavated seven municipalities dating back 800 years, though legend links the founding of Delhi to the ancient heroes of the *Mahabharata* 5,000 years ago.

Old Delhi served as the capital of Muslim India for most of the 12th through 19th centuries. Many of the city's mosques, forts, and bazaars date to the mid-17th century. In contrast, present-day New Delhi is a city of broad boulevards, landscaped gardens, and neoclassical buildings. The imperial city is a creation of the British, who began its construction in 1911 and inaugurated it as the capital of India in 1931. Today, the city is part of the Delhi Union Territory, a federal district similar to Washington, D.C.

The British came to India as traders, though they were not the first Europeans to establish trading posts in India. They were preceded by the Portuguese, French, and Dutch. It was under the hegemony of the London-based East India Company that the British established spheres of influence in Chennai (Madras) in the South, Mumbai (Bombay) in the West, and Kolkata (Calcutta) in the East. By the beginning of the 19th century, the London-based East India Company virtually ruled India.

The British captured Delhi in 1803. During the Indian Mutiny of 1857–58, Delhi was a center of resistance to the British, and the city was ransacked. The uprising, in which thousands were killed, ended the East India Company's dominance and led to its dissolution. Soon afterwards, India formally became a part of the British Empire, and a Viceroy was appointed to represent the Queen. British rule was administered from Kolkata during that early period.

In 1877, Queen Victoria was proclaimed Empress of India in Delhi. George V came to India to be crowned emperor in 1911. It was he who suggested that the Indian style be incorporated into the new imperial city to be built at New Delhi so that Indians could identify with it.

Jama Masjid (mosque), the largest mosque in India. Old Delhi. 1644–58.

At the center of New Delhi is the Presidential Palace, the Rashtrapati Bhawan. The red sandstone mansion is built in the classical style, but its huge central rotunda resembles a Buddhist *stupa* more than a Roman dome. Its 340 rooms are arranged around a dozen courtyards and once required 2,000 people for its upkeep. When completed in 1929, the cost was more than 12 million pounds. It was in Durbar Hall where the imperial throne is located that Lord Mountbatten, the last British viceroy, granted India its independence at the stroke of midnight of August 14–15, 1947. Jawaharlal Nehru became India's first prime minister.

Safdarjang Tomb. New Delhi. A.D. 1753–54.

Until recently, the Nehru family had provided all the major prime ministers of India: Nehru, his daughter Indira Gandhi (who was no relation to Mahatma Gandhi), and her son Rajiv. Both of the Gandhis were assassinated while in office in reprisal for the actions they took to solve difficult political situations. Rajiv's Italian wife Sonia, has become an important political figure.

The dichotomy of modern India is mirrored in the striking differences between Old Delhi's bazaars and New Delhi's fashionable Connaught Place. The narrow steets of Old Delhi were often jammed with people browsing at small shops and street markets. Each section of the bazaar had its unique smell. Had I been blindfolded, I could have detected the newly dyed cotton textiles or overripe fruits. I loved the aroma of the spice markets, and best of all was passing by a shop where my favorite sandalwood incense was burning.

There was seldom enough room for pedestrians in the bazaars during peak periods. They were particularly crowded in the evenings, and it was impossible not to be jostled. When an automobile or rickshaw passed, we all had to scamper out of its way, standing as close as possible to buildings, whose walls delineated the streets.

What I remember most about New Delhi is Connaught Place. Anyone who goes there will remember the typically British-looking architecture, the graceful colonnades, the huge traffic circles, and the radial roads that originate from them.

◁ *Opposite*
Iron pillar, perhaps 2,000 years old, which has never rusted. Legend says that if you can encircle it with your arms while standing with your back to it, your wish will come true. Qutub Minar Complex, Mehrauli, South Delhi.

A bicycle rickshaw driver taking children home after school. Their book bags are on top. New Delhi.

Loaded camels passing behind the Taj Mahal, as viewed from across the Yamuna River near the Agra Fort. Agra.

Agra: The Taj Mahal—Jewel of the East

One of India's finest trains, the air-conditioned and superfast Shatabdi Express, links Delhi to Agra. The 125-mile journey takes only two hours, and the train leaves Delhi early in the morning for the convenience of tourists making a day trip.

Agra was the capital of India during the Mughal rule in the 16th and 17th centuries, and I was eager to visit Agra's magnificent monuments which date from that era. The city is located on the west bank of the Yamuna River. In addition to the Taj Mahal and Agra Fort, the city has several impressive Muslim tombs. In order to visit the tombs, I hired a motor rickshaw for the remainder of the day. To reach the tomb of Emperor Akbar the Great, we had to cross over the Yamuna River on a narrow bridge. A steady flow of cars, rickshaws, bullock carts, and pedestrians resulted in a continual traffic jam.

The red sandstone mausoleum of Akbar, which was completed in 1613, was impressive. Four imposing gates lead to the grounds. One gate has Muslim motifs, one has Hindu, one has Christian, and one has Akbar's creative mixture.

Akbar was a complex individual. He came to the throne at the age of 14 when his father died. Though he never learned to read or write, he is said to have remembered every word read to him. He took drawing lessons as a boy and developed a great appreciation for art. He enjoyed the outdoors and had a fondness for dangerous sports such as elephant fighting, yet he loved music and poetry.

Even though a Muslim, Akbar had a Hindu guru and was tolerant of other religions, including Jainism, Christianity, and Zoroastrianism, a religion based on the teachings of Zarathustra from Persia. He rejected traditional Islam and founded a new religion (Din-i-Illali) which synthesized wisdom from all the major religions. Without Akbar's tolerance to his non-Muslim subjects, the success of the Mughal empire would not have been possible. Though Hindus and Muslims were not interested in his idealistic attempts to promote religious unity, his deserted royal city, Fatehpur Sikri, remains a memorial to his noble effort.

After leaving Akbar's tomb, I returned to Agra to visit the squat mausoleum of Itimad-ud-Daula. The short minarets at each of the tomb's four corners foreshadowed elements which would reach perfection in the design of the Taj. The Persian buried here was the emperor's chief minister. His beautiful daughter married Emperor Jahangir, son of Emperor Akbar, and she became known as Nur Jahan, the "light of the world."

I waited until late afternoon to visit the Taj Mahal. The world-famous Mughal monument was erected by Emperor Shah Jahan in memory of his beautiful wife Mumtaz Mahal, who died in childbirth in 1629, three years after he came to the throne, after having given him 14 children, only seven of whom survived.

Shah Jahan, whose title means "King of the World," has the reputation of being the greatest builder of all the Indian emperors. Construction of the Taj employed 20,000 workers from India and Central Asia and took 22 years. It was completed in 1653. The scaffolding supposedly cost as much as the structure due to lack of wood, necessitating that it be made of stone. The main architect came from Shiraz in Iran, and artisans were brought from France and Italy to assist with the decoration.

It is said that Shah Jahan had intended to build a second Taj in black marble across the river for his own tomb, a negative image of the white Taj. But before he could embark on this project, he was deposed by his son Aurangzeb, just as Shah Jahan had done to his father, Jahangir. Shah Jahan spent the rest of his life as a prisoner in the Agra Fort, looking across the river at his lavish memorial to his favorite wife.

The Taj Mahal is one of the most beautifully proportioned buildings in the world and retains its symmetry from any angle. It reduces Persian and Indian styles to an elegant and simple form. The building's details are also impressive, with inlaid semi-precious stones forming designs in a process known as *pietra dura*. Like the Grand Canyon in Arizona, the Taj looks different with the changing light, and even though I had seen many pictures of it, standing in its presence was exhilarating.

The next day I went to the Agra Fort, which was begun by Akbar in 1565. The huge fort, with its red sandstone walls, looked similar to the Red Fort at Old Delhi. Initially a military edifice, it became more luxurious by the time of Shah Jahan's reign. The fort's marble Moti Masjid (Pearl Mosque) was built by Shah Jahan between 1631–53. It is considered to be perfectly proportioned, and a Persian inscription inside the mosque compares it to a flawless pearl.

Taj Mahal at sunrise as seen from across the Yamuna River. Agra.

Mathura and Vrindavan (Brindaban), Uttar Pradesh

Mathura

Located close to Agra are the holy cities of Mathura and Vrindavan (Brindaban). Both municipalities are located on the bank of the sacred Yamuna River and were sanctified by the presence of Krishna during his early life. Many Hindus consider Krishna to be India's greatest human expression of Divinity, and they cherish the anecdotes of his mischievous childhood.

Legend has it that Krishna's parents were held captive in a prison, where the infant was born over 3,500 years ago. They had been imprisoned because of a prophecy that they would give birth to a son who would grow up to overthrow the evil king Kansa. All of their children were put to death at birth, but Krishna miraculously survived. The story closely parallels the prophecy of the birth of Jesus and the Slaughter of the Innocent, in which Herod massacred guiltless children for similar reasons.

Mathura has a long history of multiculturalism. Prior to the arrival of the Buddhists of the Kushan dynasty from northern India almost 2,000 years ago, the city had been a religious center to the Jains. Buddhism continued to flourish in Mathura with the rise of the powerful new Gupta Empire in about A.D. 320.

I hired a boat for a short ride on the Yamuna River. The trip afforded an excellent view of the temples and bathing *ghats*, which were almost deserted so late in the morning.

The site of the Kesava Deo Temple, built on the spot where Lord Krishna is said to have been born, is covered by a mosque erected in 1661. I was told by my guide that in keeping with the tradition of Muslim conquests at that time, the sacred Hindu temple was destroyed and a mosque was constructed in its place. Hindus are allowed to worship in a simple basement shrine. Although there was little to see, I could feel strong spiritual vibrations. Perhaps the sanctity of the spot was permeated by Krishna himself and had been enhanced by the devotion of millions of pious Hindu pilgrims.

Vrindavan (Brindaban)

Vrindavan, with its famous temples dedicated to Lord Krishna, is located about six miles north of Mathura. This is where the mischievous child Krishna played tricks on the *gopis* (milkmaids), and it is a favorite pilgrimage site for Hindus. When we arrived, there were several busloads of pilgrims who had made the long, arduous trip from Nepal. They had come to honor Krishna, whose Bhagavad Gita is the most beloved scripture of Hindus.

A shrine of the Goddess of the Yamuna River. Vrindavan (Brindaban).

Krishna brought essentially the same teachings to the East that Christ later brought to the West. The central message of the Bhagavad Gita is that men and women may attain liberation through love for God, wisdom, and performance of right actions in the spirit of non-attachment.

Non-attachment does not mean indifference. To be non-attached is to do our very best enthusiastically and to try our hardest, regardless of the circumstances or what others may think or say. Krishna counsels his disciple Arjuna that giving credit to God for the results, or "fruits," of our actions, whether success or failure, is the correct attitude to have while performing our daily duties. By dedicating all work to God and letting Him be responsible for the outcome, we acknowledge that He is the doer, not us. This enables us to live in the moment, performing each action for the joy of doing the right thing. It also helps us to loosen the grip of our ego.

Hindus believe that being attached to the results of our actions keeps us tied to our *karma*, both good and bad, making it impossible to break the cords that bind us to human existence (reincarnation). Thus, Krishna said to Arjuna, "The God-united yogi, abandoning attachment to fruits of actions, attains the peace unshakable" (Bhagavad Gita V:12).

A woman drying a sari on the bank of the Yamuna River.
Vrindavan (Brindaban), Uttar Pradesh.

Even-Mindedness

Non-attachment leads to even-mindedness. "To be even-minded is to be always anchored in God. It is to live in His peace within as we pass through life—dealing effectively with every situation that arises, without becoming emotionally ruffled."[1] Until we can deal with all dualities of the finite world, such as war and peace, sickness and health, wealth and poverty, and remain unaffected by them, we still have a major spiritual lesson to learn. That is what Krishna meant when he said to Arjuna:

> O, Arjuna! he who cannot be ruffled by these (contacts of the
> senses with their objects), who is calm and even-minded during
> pain and pleasure, he alone is fit to attain everlastingness!
> —Bhagavad Gita II:15

On my most recent trip to India, I was in Vrindavan (Brindaban) during the second day of the Spring festival of Holi. Hardly anyone escapes being sprinkled with colored water and powders, so it is wise not to wear good clothing during that period. Some say that the holiday's tradition of playfully throwing colored powders on others stems from similar pranks that young Krishna played on *gopis* (milkmaids) over 3,500 years ago.

Being in the midst of so many devoted village pilgrims was both uplifting and fun. They seemed to delight in tossing colored powders on everyone, including me. I noticed the children preferred to use the modern technology of squirt guns, which give them a maximum range to spray their colored water. For me, the day came to a close all too soon.

Opposite ▷
A statue of Krishna in a tree where he tied the clothing of the bathing gopis (milkmaids). Requiring them to appear naked before him is symbolic of our having to shed all of our external coverings before our soul can stand "naked" before God. Vrindavan (Brindaban).

Pilgrims during the festival of Holi. Note the purple powder tossed in the air in the background. Vrindavan (Brindaban).

A woman performing prayers in the holy Ganges River. Varanasi (Banaras), Uttar Pradesh.

Early morning along the Ganges River. Note the praying women holding lighted candles. Varanasi (Banaras).

Hindu Golden Temple. In the background are the towering minarets of a mosque. Varanasi (Banaras).

The Holy City of Varanasi (Banaras)

On my overnight coach to Varanasi (Banaras), I met two female students who were completing their last year of studies at Varanasi University. Both planned to do social work after graduating. Prior to arriving in Varanasi, I asked if it were appropriate to take them to dinner one evening. After discussing the matter in their own language, they accepted, and a time was fixed.

When I went to meet them at their dormitory the next evening, they were outside, waiting for me. I noticed a large group of young ladies standing nearby. They were residents of the dormitory who had assembled to see their two friends' "date." I was surprised that even though they were 21 years old, they had to be back at the dormitory for a 7:30 p.m. curfew for girls.

Varanasi, the holiest and most beloved city of the Hindus, has been known by several names. The city once was called Kashi, but today it is known by its ancient Indian name Varanasi, which means "the city between two rivers." Built on the banks of the sacred Ganges, it is one of India's most important pilgrimage sites. It has been a center of learning for over 2,000 years. Located only six miles away is Sarnath, where the Buddha preached his first sermon. To Hindus, Varanasi is considered an auspicious place to die.

Varanasi's principal attraction is the continuous line of bathing *ghats* built on the west bank of the Ganges. There are over 100 *ghats* whose steps leading down to the river facilitate the pilgrims' performance of their ritual purification. Similarly, Christians are baptized in the River Jordan.

Dawn was approaching as I arrived at a bathing *ghat* from which I could hire a boat for an early-morning ride on the Ganges. The trip was fascinating. The river's edge offered glimpses of many aspects of daily life. Some Hindus were performing rituals, while others were bathing or washing clothes.

Male pilgrims receiving prasad *(divinely blessed sweets) from a priest at a* ghat. *Varanasi (Banaras).*

A monk sitting on the steps of a ghat *after his bath, applying religious markings to forehead. Varanasi (Banaras).*

What impressed me most about the many pilgrims was their devotion, which their facial expressions clearly mirrored. The cold morning air and water temperature did not chill their faith.

In the afternoon, I went to the Durga Temple, commonly called the Monkey Temple due to the many monkeys who have made it their home. Before leaving for India, an American woman who had previously visited the country told me of a frightening incident. She had been chased by a band of vicious monkeys one afternoon when visiting a temple. She escaped by jumping onto a stone in a nearby stream and waiting there until the monkeys left. I accepted her fear into my consciousness and hoped nothing like that would happen to me.

Fortunately, I was told another story about monkeys prior to my departure. It involved the early life of Swami Vivekananda, the chief disciple of the yogic master Sri Ramakrishna. When walking down a street of Varanasi, he was followed by one monkey and then another. He became frightened, and the faster he walked, the more interested the monkeys became. The number increased until he was followed by a large troup.

As he hurriedly rounded a corner trying to escape, he passed a *sadhu* sitting peacefully in meditation. Swami Vivekananda shouted to him, "What should I do?" The ascetic answered, "Face the brutes." He did, and the whole troupe turned and fled.

After hearing that story and realizing that monkeys were cowards, I was no longer afraid of them. As a result, I enjoyed all of my encounters with them—even the pesky ones. On several occasions, I would playfully scold the aggressive ones for their unbecoming behavior, and invariably they turned and went away.

Opposite ▷

Male pilgrims bathing in the Ganges River. The women on the steps are drying saris. Varanasi (Banaras), Uttar Pradesh.

A sunken temple. Ganges River.
Varanasi (Banaras), Uttar Pradesh.

A boat with pilgrims emerging from an early morning fog on the Ganges River. Varanasi (Banaras).

The Great Mosque of Aurangzeb as seen from the Ganges River. Varanasi (Banaras).

Sarnath

Early the next morning, I went to Sarnath. It was there at the Deer Park that the Buddha preached his first sermon to his fellow ascetics after having achieved enlightenment at Bodh Gaya.

The excavations at Sarnath are extensive. In addition to a large restored *stupa* believed to date from about A.D. 500, the ruins include foundations of many early Buddhist buildings which are over 1,500 years old. Two Chinese travelers who visited the site in A.D. 640. recorded that the colony had over 1,500 priests and a *stupa* nearly 300 feet high. They also saw an imposing pillar over 60 feet high erected by Ashoka, the great emperor and patron of Buddhism. The famous lion capital from the remnants of the Ashokan pillar, circa 250 B.C., is still in pristine condition. The highly polished fluted capital may be seen in the local museum. The Ashokan symbol of four back-to-back lions is the symbol of modern India.

Sarnath's excellent Archaeological Museum also contains perhaps the most sublime example of Gupta sculpture. The magnificently carved 5th century sandstone Buddha is seated as a yogi on a throne. His hands perform a *mudra* (formal gesture), symbolizing that he is preaching the Buddhist Law. His upper body is backed by a huge, intricately decorated halo with two heavenly beings flying at the top, celebrating the first sermon at Sarnath.

Buddhism was already in decline when the destructive Muslim invasions began. Sarnath was not spared, and its buildings were destroyed and desecrated. Even the usually tolerant Akbar built a monument to his father over one of the *stupas*.

As sunset approached, I returned to Varanasi (Banaras). The peaceful feeling I experienced at Sarnath was so strong that I made a vow to visit the Buddha's birthplace in present-day Nepal. It was then that I realized one of my purposes for coming to India—to receive the vibrations of the Great Ones.

I also visited Kushinagar, another important Buddhist pilgrimage site. It is located about 140 miles north of Varanasi, near Gorakhpur, which is close to the neighboring country of Nepal. Kushinagar is thought to be the place where the Buddha died and entered into *nirvana*.

A pilgrim, Gorakhnath Temple. Gorakhpur.

Buddhist pilgrims circling the Dhamekh Stupa. Height: 111 feet. Sarnath. ca. A.D. 500.

Pilgrims being ferried to the confluence of the Yamuna and the Ganges rivers for a holy dip. An estimated 19–20 million people, a portion of them seen in the background, attended during the most auspicious 24-hour period. Kumbha Mela. *Allahabad. February 6, 1989.*

The Kumbha Mela *at Allahabad*

The *Kumbha Mela* represents the heart and soul of India. For thousands of years, saints and sages have come from the Himalayan Mountains and forests to attend this ancient festival, thereby keeping spiritual goals in constant sight of the ordinary people. Tens of millions of devout Hindus gather here every 12 years to purify themselves in the Ganges River and to mingle with the thousands of *sadhus*, yogis, swamis, and ascetics of all types. Many are hermits who leave their secluded abodes only to attend the *melas*, where they bestow their blessings upon the multitudes. There are many impostors and hypocrites, but "For the faults of the many, judge not the whole. Everything on earth is of mixed character. Though many *sadhus* here still wander in delusion, yet the *mela* is blessed by a few men of God-realization."[2]

The site of the gathering at Allahabad is the vast expanse of land located on both sides of two of India's most important rivers—the Ganges and the Yamuna. Hindus believe bathing at the *sangam*, the confluence, gives special purification. The *sangam* is even more sacred because it is believed that a third river, the ancient Sarasvati, that has since dried up and gone underground, once merged there.

The *Kumbha Mela* is the largest religious festival in the world. On auspicious astrological days, the surging crowds swell to over 27 million! It was on one of those four special days that I arrived in Allahabad. As I neared the *Kumbha Mela* grounds, thousands of people were entering and leaving. My rickshaw driver insisted on dropping me at the main gate to avoid having to deal with the congestion inside. I was now on my own to find a small plot of land which was the camp where I would be staying.

My home for the next three days was surrounded by an ocean of humanity, and I had forgotten to bring its plot designation with me! I began walking with the flow of pedestrians, not knowing where I was going.

Kumbha Mela, *Allahabad, Uttar Pradesh*

I passed through the arch of a large wooden gate, marking the formal entrance to the *mela's* grounds. A thrill went through me as I thought of all the sacred feet which had trod this path before me. Although it took me about three hours to find my camp, I was grateful to have arrived at all.

After having a simple dinner, I toured the grounds and visited other *ashrams*. One organization had neon displays of scenes from the scriptures. The one that got the most attention was that of a god shooting an arrow whose trajectory found its mark in the chest of a villain. Though the lectures at our camp were given in Hindi, someone translated parts of them for me. One of the points that impressed me was: "Life is a school. Do not look for happiness here. It will come later." Said another way, "The things that happen to us do not matter; what we become through them does."[3] When I later asked the monk to elaborate on what he meant, he replied, "If we become ruffled, remember that it is God who is arranging those circumstances to show us our ego." I think all religions agree that "When the 'I' shall die, then shall I know who am I."

Because of snows in the Himalayas, the nights were extremely cold. I bought an extra wool blanket and slept in my warmest clothes. I noticed some peasants sleeping on the ground in lightweight clothing. Many had only cotton blankets, and some had no coverings at all. Devotion!

The camp directly across from ours used a loudspeaker at an ear-piercing volume. The speaker system blared 15 to 17 hours a day as various persons of all ages evidently gave testimonials praising God. When a Westerner complained about the noise to an Indian, he responded: "If you understood what they are saying, you would not say that." From that moment, I had a new attitude towards the noise produced by so many people.

That afternoon, I was invited to join a group who hired a large boat to go to the *sangam* (confluence) to bathe. There were hundreds of similar boats ferrying pilgrims to the auspicious spot. Several Hindus wished me well while I was in the water and appreciated my honoring their rituals. I was unable to see the banks because of the vast numbers of bathers.

Visiting the *Kumbha Mela* was especially memorable. It helped me to pierce the shroud of that country's mystique and to intimately witness its outpouring of devotion.

Pilgrims at the Kumbha Mela. *Allahabad. February 6, 1989.*

An ascetic. The trident in the foreground and the sacred ashes smeared on his body signify that he is a devotee of Shiva. Kumbha Mela. *Allahabad.*

A portion of an estimated 19–20 million pilgrims who bathed in the river during the auspicious 24-hour period. Kumbha Mela. *Allahabad. February 6, 1989.*

A parade of sadhus *en route to the river to bathe.* Kumbha Mela. *Allahabad.*

Kumbha Mela, *Allahabad, Uttar Pradesh*

The Kumbha Mela *grounds become a tent city. Early morning. Allahabad.*

Swamis, in orange robes, walking on the Kumbha Mela *grounds. Early morning. Allahabad. February 6, 1989.*

A shrine commemorating Paramahansa Yogananda. Yogoda Satsanga camp. Kumbha Mela. Allahabad.

Pilgrims gathered for evening prayers along the Ganges River. Har ki Pairi ghat. Hardwar.

Hardwar: Gateway to Heaven

Hardwar is one of my favorite places in India. Located in the foothills of the Himalayas where the Ganges River begins its flow across the plains, it can be reached from Delhi in only six hours by bus or a little longer by overnight train.

No trip to India is complete without visiting Hardwar's Har ki Pairi *ghat* in the evening. Hundreds of pilgrims sing evening prayers, while priests on the opposite bank ritually wave flaming lamps (*arati*). Many pilgrims release small "leaf boats," containing flowers and a lighted candle, into the swiftly-flowing river. I loved the inspiring *arati* ceremony so much that I went to Hardwar often.

The holy water of the Ganges River has the extraordinary—if not unique—feature of its unpollutability. Evidently, no bacteria can live in its changeless sterility—a fact that baffles modern scientists. Not surprisingly, pilgrims consider the river's water sacred. Bathing there is considered most auspicious.

An abstract image of a deity.
Mansa Devi Temple. Hardwar.

Priests with flaming lamps performing arati *along the Ganges River. Har ki Pairi ghat. Hardwar.*

A basket containing "leaf boats." Har ki Pairi ghat. *Hardwar.*

A woman placing a "leaf boat" with a lighted candle in the Ganges River. Har ki Pairi ghat. Hardwar.

Local people bathing on a holy day at the confluence of the Bhagirathi and Alaknanda rivers, where the Ganges River begins. Garhwal Himalayas. Devprayag, Uttaranchal.

Shivling Peak, 21,000 feet high, is the mythological source of the Ganges River. Garhwal Himalayan Mountains, Gaumukh vicinity, Gangotri region.

Yamunotri, Gangotri, Kedarnath, and Badrinath

Located northeast of Rishikesh in an area known as the Garhwal Himalayas are four sacred Hindu pilgrimage sites. Yamunotri is at the source of the Yamuna (Jamuna) River, and Gangotri is near the glacial origin of the Ganges at Gaumukh. The mountaintop temple at Kedarnath is situated at the base of an impressive snow-covered peak at an altitude of 11,750 feet. From the town below, the temple can only be reached by foot, horseback, or in a chair carried up the steep terrain supported on the shoulders of four men. Badrinath is dedicated to Lord Vishnu and is accessible by car or bus. Near Badrinath is Joshimath, where there is a sacred cave once used by the philosopher-saint Shankara when he journeyed to Badrinath on foot in the 8th century.

To visit the four remote Himalayan pilgrimage sites, I took a 12-day bus tour. I was the only foreigner on the pilgrimage, and the group of about 20 Hindus adopted me and made sure that I was as comfortable as the rustic circumstances allowed. Each morning immediately before the bus began the day's journey, they would shout an affirmation to God in unison. It was very inspiring.

The night before we made the trip to Kedarnath, the women prepared a special meal. Because it was raining and muddy, I had on old clothes. To my embarrassment, when I entered the small kitchen to eat, all the women had on fine saris, many of which had gold embroidery on the bottom edge. They had brought them especially for this occasion to honor God on the evening before our sacred ascent and were not the least concerned about ruining their finest saris in the mud.

It is said that all who make the pilgrimage to Kedarnath and Badrinath will be brother and sister disciples for life. I would agree. Our group had a great camaraderie, and by the end of the trip, we were like a large family.

To make the pilgrimage to these temples is an act of faith. The narrow mountain roads are so dangerous that I am surprised there are not more collisions involving buses. Our driver was excellent, although I cannot say the same of the others. Because of snow and monsoon rains, roads are only open during the summer and early fall. On my trip, which was during the end of the monsoon in mid-September, the rains made the mountains lush and green. However, a landslide prevented us from reaching Yamunotri.

Badrinath Temple.

Kedarnath Temple.

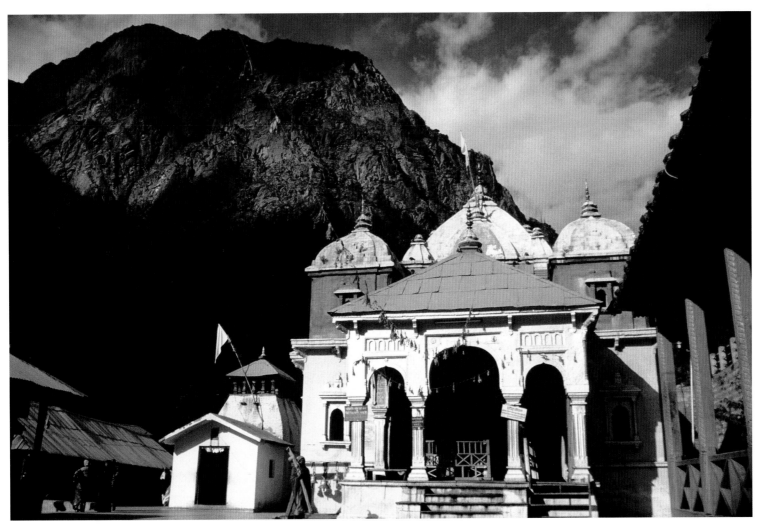

A temple dedicated to the goddess Ganga. Gangotri. Early 18th century.

*A woman with
her children.
Dwarahat.*

*Women carrying
fodder.
Dwarahat.*

Dwarahat

About 100 miles south of Badrinath is the small Himalayan town of Dwarahat. I was making a pilgrimage to a cave once inhabited by an *avatar* known as Babaji (Reverend Father).

It was cold and dark when I finally arrived at my destination, a small *ashram* built on a hill outside of Dwarahat. The next morning, after a simple breakfast, a monk from the *ashram* led me to the cave.

When we returned, the monk told me some parables. Several of the allegories were from the *shastras* (sacred books) and contained profound truths under a veil of detailed symbolism from the *Puranas*. They related to the importance of keeping one's word. The following story had a deep impact on me:[4]

Once, a beautiful pigeon pursued by a hawk dropped from the sky and sought protection from the king of Banaras. Seeing the pigeon's terror, the king said, "Be comforted, good bird. Fear not, for none need fear who seek protection here. For thy protection, I will surrender all my kingdom; yea, if need be, life itself."

The hawk challenged the king's words and said, "This bird is my appointed food. Thou shouldst not protect my lawful prey, won by hard endeavor. O king, hunger is gnawing at my stomach. Thou hast the right to intervene when human beings fight, but what lawful power hast thou over the birds that range the sky?" Then the king said, "So be it; let a bull or boar or deer be dressed for thee, for thou shalt not have the bird." But the hawk replied, "I do not eat the flesh of bulls or boars or deer. Pigeons are my appointed food. But if thou hast such affection for the pigeon, give flesh from thine own body equal to the pigeon's weight." The king agreed, and the pigeon was placed in one of the pans of a scale.

As the king began cutting off strips of his flesh, the earth shook to bear witness to his act of keeping his word. Though the king cut flesh from his arms and thighs, he filled the scale in vain, for the gods caused the pigeon to weigh heavier than the flesh. Even after stripping away all of his flesh, the scale would not budge. When the king was nothing but a skeleton, he desired to give his whole body, and stepped into the scale. Then the gods appeared, and for his joyful sacrifice to defend the weak and unprotected, they restored his body and took him away to heaven.

The story has several morals: the importance of keeping one's word; the duty of the strong to protect the weak; and God can give us some harsh tests until we prove ourselves worthy. In other words, our belief in God must be tested to prove its value.

One of Shakespeare's most well-known plays, *The Merchant of Venice*, has a similar plot which requires a merchant to forfeit a pound of flesh for his failure to fulfill the terms of a financial contract. It is interesting to note that the play's primary message—the importance of keeping one's word—has been overlooked in favor of lesser themes.

Throughout the ages, the ideal of truth (*satya*) has permeated Hindu society. Hindu scriptures proclaim that those who habitually speak only the truth develop the power of materializing their words. "What commands they utter from the heart come to pass" (*Yoga Sutras* II:36). Marco Polo said of his travels to India that the priests "would not utter a lie for anything on earth." In the annals of English judges and administrators during the British colonial period, one judge wrote, "I have had before me hundreds of cases in which a man's property, liberty, or life depended on his telling a lie, and he has refused to tell it."

Pilgrims crossing Gurus' Bridge to Harmandir Sahib (Golden Temple). Early morning. Amritsar.

Harmandir Sahib (Golden Temple), Amritsar

The holy city of Amritsar was founded in 1577 and is only 16 miles from the border of Pakistan. The Harmandir Sahib, the Sikhs' holiest shrine, is located there. The city was sacked by a Mughal emperor in 1761, and the temple was destroyed. It was rebuilt in 1764, and in 1802 the roof was covered with gilded copper plates. Ever since, it has been popularly known as the Golden Temple.

The two-story marble temple sits regally in a large, sacred pool from which Amritsar (Pool of Immortality-

giving Nectar) received its name. The temple is a blend of Hindu and Muslim architectural styles and is reached by a marble causeway known as Gurus' Bridge.

I covered my head and washed my feet in the wading pool, as all are required to do. Crossing the crowded, narrow causeway, I entered the temple. Inside, a priest was reading from the original copy of the Sikhs' holy book, the Granth Sahib, which contains the tenets from the 10 Sikh gurus, as well as Hindu and Muslim writings. The readings and singings of the hymns are broadcast by loudspeakers and resonate within the walls of the huge compound. A male singer was accompanied by a harmonium, my favorite Indian instrument. I found the chanting so uplifting that one afternoon I sat on the upper floor of the temple and listened to the enrapturing music for hours.

Harmandir Sahib (Golden Temple). Amritsar.

Opposite ▷

A priest waving a fly whisk to ritually fan the original copy of the Sikh holy book, the Granth Sahib, covered with embroidered cloth. Harmandir Sahib (Golden Temple). Amritsar.

Sikh men attending evening prayers. Harmandir Sahib (Golden Temple), upper floor. Amritsar.

The Sikh religion was founded in 1469 by the God-realized Guru Nanak, who was revered by both Hindus and Muslims. He espoused the best of both religions and made a conscious attempt to harmonize the two most powerful rival religions of India. To this day, Guru Nanak is venerated by the Sikhs, Hindus, and Muslims and offers an enduring testimonial to the power of divine love.

One of the concepts of the Sikhs is *Guru Ka Langar* (common kitchen), which was established to abolish caste distinction. Nearly all Sikh temples have a community kitchen where volunteers prepare free meals for pilgrims. At the Harmandir Sahib (Golden Temple) in Amritsar, thousands of people are fed daily. Sikh temples also provide free accommodations to all at *gurdwaras* (guest houses) located nearby.

In an attempt to halt Muslim persecution and atrocities, military overtones were introduced into the Sikh religion during the 17th century. Several of the Sikh gurus transformed their followers into a formidable military force which successfully fought the Mughal Islamic rulers of India. It was the last Sikh guru, Guru Govind Singh (1675–1708), who founded the *Khalsa*, the militant Sikh theocracy. He required all Sikhs to assume the surname Singh, meaning "Lion," so they might be united to fight the religiously intolerant Mughals. Since that time, most of the Sikhs have assumed the surname Singh. However, having the name does not necessarily mean that one is a Sikh; many Rajputs have the same name.

Opposite ▷
The Harmandir Sahib (Golden Temple) at night. Amritsar, Punjab.

Houseboats on Dal Lake. Srinagar.

The Mountain Paradise of Kashmir

Many travelers think Kashmir is the most beautiful region in the world. Its green valleys and beautiful lakes, serenely guarded by the snow-capped Himalayas, have earned it the name of "Little Switzerland." As I stepped off the plane and inhaled a deep breath of refreshing mountain air, I understood why its cool climate has long made it a retreat from the heat of the Indian plains. I was looking forward to a much-needed rest.

Kashmir was not originally a part of British India. It was a princely state whose ruler got to choose whether he wanted to join India or Pakistan. L. Collins and D. Lapierre's *Freedom at Midnight* relates how the maharaja's indecisive action led to a Pakistani invasion which resulted in the first Indo-Pakistani conflict. The region is now divided, with approximately two-thirds belonging to India and one-third to Pakistan, but both countries claim it all.

Houseboats serve as hotels for tourists. Dal Lake. Srinagar.

The current political turmoil in Kashmir is symptomatic of both India's and the world's challenge to preserve national and global unity. Various minority cultures in India want to establish their own independent countries, claiming they were once separate political units. Such arguments are clearly untenable to the Indian central government. Indians of different religions and ethnic groups will just have to learn to get along with each other! The creation of the modern states of Pakistan and India have proven that separating people by religion is not the solution to global peace.

Srinagar

Srinagar, the capital of Kashmir, was founded in the third century B.C. by Emperor Ashoka. He constructed 500 monasteries there, of which 100 still stood 1,000 years later.

The city is built on Dal Lake, which is the scenic state's greatest attraction. Portions of the lake are afloat with houseboats, where one can sit on a veranda and forget the worries of the world.

The houseboats were the ingenious idea of the British, who were not allowed to own land there during the British colonial period. My houseboat consisted of a Victorian living room, a dining room, and two bedrooms, each with modern Western bathrooms. The owner, Mohammed, lived in an adjacent houseboat. Every morning, he would ask me what foods and fresh vegetables I would like prepared for my meals. After I got to know him better, he invited me to eat breakfast with his family, but preferred to serve me lunch and dinner in my more luxurious quarters.

One of the more enjoyable experiences in Srinagar is riding through the maze of peaceful waterways on a *shikara*, one of the long, graceful boats which ply the lakes. A deluxe *shikara* has a canopy and thick-cushioned "full spring seats" which make the leisurely trip comfortable.

The Mughal rulers of India also appreciated Kashmir. Akbar built a fort on a hill overlooking the city, and it makes a scenic

Men relaxing in front of a shop smoking a hookah (water pipe). Dal Lake. Srinagar.

backdrop. Formal gardens, whose style was refined to an art by the Mughal kings, are well maintained. The Shalimar Gardens, built by Jahangir for his wife, had some of the most beautiful roses I have ever seen. For a small tip, the gardeners delighted in cutting any roses that the tourists wanted.

A mother with her children, paddling a boat. Dal Lake. Srinagar.

Jammu and Kashmir

Roses. Dal Lake. Srinagar.

Sixty miles from Srinagar is the town of Pahalgam. It is built on the narrow, fast-flowing Lidder River, whose blue-green water is filled with moss-laden boulders. I stayed at a hotel which was so near the river that its rushing waters lulled me to sleep at night. What a pleasure it was to awake each morning greeted by the river's salutation. The early morning sunlight illuminated the fir-covered, snow-capped mountains which were silhouetted against a blue sky. The Cosmic Artist was at it again!

The mountain air was so invigorating that I decided to hike to some nearby towns. Loading a small backpack with as few necessities as possible, I walked about eight miles along the Lidder River to the little village of Aru. I spent the night there and continued to Lidderwat the next day. My four-hour hike took me through spectacular mountain scenery. Many shepherds had brought their flocks of sheep to the high meadows for the summer.

After returning to Srinagar, I took a bus to Gulmarg, less than 35 miles away. The small valley was ringed by intimidating mountains, giving the impression that one was a prisoner of nature.

My hotel was on a steep hill. The lushness of the valley's rolling green hills gave the appearance of springtime. A dense forest growing on the side of the mountain was partially shrouded by mist. Floating clusters of white clouds concealed patches of the tall, timbered sentinels higher up the precipice. Above the clouds, the trees reappeared, forming an abrupt contrast to the dark, barren, snow-capped bluffs higher up. Frozen rivers of snow extending down the slopes would thaw later on and send water to the valley below. Light and dark clouds concealed the setting sun, providing celestial backlighting for the magnificent view. It seemed a shame that nature's tranquility could not be shared by its human inhabitants.

A man poling a shikara *loaded with weeds cleared from Dal Lake. Srinagar.*

The towering Karakoram mountain range, 20,000 to 23,000 feet high, allows less than 4 inches of rain per year. Ladakh.

Tikse Gompa (monastery). Ladakh.

Ladakh

I had heard so many exotic stories about Ladakh from travelers that I was eager to visit the old kingdom. Ladakh is about the size of England and is located high in the Himalayan Mountains, due east of and contiguous with Kashmir. The area often is called "Little Tibet." Its people, culture, and Tantric Buddhist religion and monasteries are a microcosm of what Tibet was like before the Chinese invaded.

Ladakh has one of the highest elevations of any inhabited region in the world. It also has one of the most arid climates, as the colossal Karakoram Mountains allow less than four inches of rainfall annually. Most of its elevated mountains are completely devoid of plant life, which prompts many travelers to compare the rugged terrain to the barren landscape of the moon. Isolated from the rest of the world for about eight months a year, Ladakh's high plateau could be Shangri-la from the movie *Lost Horizons*.

Ladakh is part of the modern Indian state of Jammu and Kashmir, which is predominantly Muslim. The 45,000 square miles of Ladakhi desert constitute the greater part of the region. The Buddhist majority of Ladakh want to be formally separated from the pro-Muslim government. To further complicate the political situation, the Chinese invaded Ladakh in 1962, and today the Sino-Indian border remains a militarized zone.

My 30-minute flight from Srinagar over the snow-covered mountain peaks was impressive. The airport is on a hilltop overlooking the Indus River. At the end of the runway, the 1,000-year-old Spitok Gompa (monastery) welcomes travelers to another world.

Buddhist monks chanting prayers during a ceremony. Tikse Gompa (monastery). Ladakh, Jammu and Kashmir.

Tikse

Tikse Gompa (monastery) is about 10 miles from Leh. Its numerous white-washed buildings sprawl down the side of a barren, rocky mountain.

The path winding up the steep hill to the Tikse monastery did not look intimidating, but because I was not acclimated to the high altitudes, I had to stop several times during my climb to catch my breath. It is not uncommon for visitors to Leh to have splitting headaches for the first 24 hours until their bodies adjust to an altitude of over 10,500 feet, and I was no exception.

When I reached the top, a Buddhist ceremony was in progress. Many of the monks were gathered in a courtyard. An old monk, whom I assume was in charge of the monastery, was wearing a crown and a ceremonial robe. He was sitting in front of a fire, which probably symbolized the purifying flames which destroy one's *karma*. In his left hand, he was holding a prayer bell which he rang periodically as he intoned a chant. With two fingers of his right hand, he occasionally dropped a powdered substance into the fire, which caused bright bursts of flames to shoot upwards.

A Buddhist monk conducting a ceremony. Tikse Gompa.

Tikse Gompa (monastery). Near Leh.

A library. Old manuscripts are kept in boxes wrapped in cloth. Monastery. Nubra Valley, Ladakh.

Buddhist monk holding key to the library, standing in front of an old, carved wooden statue of a lama. Hemis Gompa. Ladakh.

A monastery school. Lekir Gompa. Ladakh.

Hemis

About 25 miles from Leh is the Hemis Gompa, one of the largest and most important monasteries in Ladakh. It would be easy to pass by this monastery if one did not know of its location because it is tucked under the summit of a steep mountain. As the site of the most famous *gompa* festival in Ladakh, it has many well-preserved wall paintings. I was eager to visit the library with its ancient manuscripts, and the monk showing me around unlocked it for me. It was at Hemis in 1887 that the Russian traveler Nicholas Notovitch persuaded a monk to show him the two books that according to Buddhist accounts recorded Jesus Christ's visit to India. The document covers Jesus' life from age 13 to 26, the major portion of his years not accounted for in the Bible. The chronicle confirms that Jesus visited the famous Jagannath Temple in Puri and other such sacred cities in India as Varanasi (Banaras). Some believe that Jesus' trip to India was to return the visit of the "three wise men from the East" who came to Bethlehem to honor His arrival on earth.

Aided by his interpreter who translated from the Tibetan language, Notovitch carefully wrote down the various verses as they were read to him. Published in 1894 as *The Unknown Life of Jesus Christ*, the account is available in English (translated from the French by V. R. Gandhi). Notovitch never doubted the document's authenticity.

The early Buddhist account of Jesus' life and death vindicated the Sanhedrin, who by Pilate's order summoned Jesus to appear before the tribunal. The Buddhist chronicle portrays sympathy between the elders of Israel and Jesus, and their findings sent to Pilate were: "We will not judge a just man." According to Notovitch, the Buddhist document makes it clear that Pilate alone was responsible for Jesus' death, not the Pharisees and the Jews. Pilate viewed Jesus' growing popularity as a threat to himself and to Rome's control over the ancient Jewish nation, and he manipulated a scenario to have Jesus put to death.

Two women winnowing barley with willow rakes to separate the grain from the chaff. Khardung. Nubra Valley, Ladakh, Jammu and Kashmir.

Ladakhi children.
Khardung, Nubra Valley,
Jammu and Kashmir.

Carved animal mask. Wood and paint. Leh Palace. 19th century. Masks, symbolizing good and evil, are worn by monks in dance ceremonies originally held for the townspeople.

Avalokiteshvara, Lord of Compassion, with 1,000 arms. Gilt wood, paint, and cloth. Monastery. Nubra Valley.

When walking through a field along the Indus River near Leh en route to a cave temple, I came upon a huge pile of *mani* stones. Each was beautifully carved with the inscription *Om mani padme hum.* The famous Tibetan chant literally means "Praise to the Jewel at the Heart of the Lotus." Its metaphysical significance affirms the brilliance of God's illumining light at the spiritual eye between the eyebrows. Evidently, the *mani* stones had been placed there as votive offerings by individuals making a pilgrimage to the same cave.

Monasteries laden with paintings and art objects place Ladakh high on my list of the world's most exotic places to visit. The people are warm and friendly. Anyone who has ever visited Ladakh will remember their big smiles and rosy cheeks and their traditional welcome *"Jullay."*

Mani *stones in a field overlooking the Indus River. Near Leh.*

The City Palace, the largest
palace complex in the state.
Udaipur, Rajasthan.

Chapter Four

Rajasthan

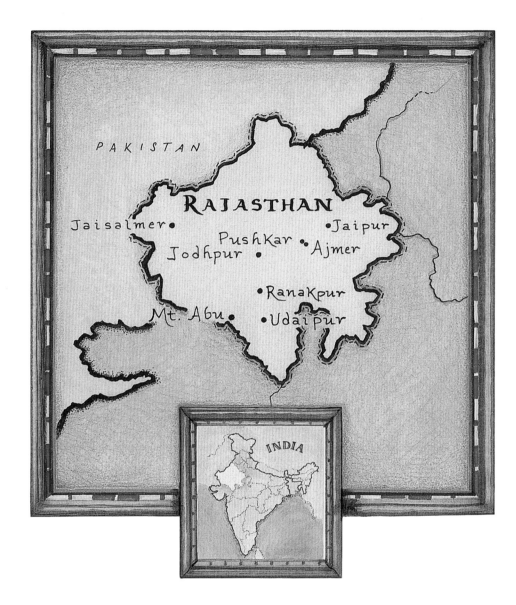

◁ *Opposite*
Water being drawn from
an oasis near Jaisalmer.

The Northwest: A Sojourn to Exotic Rajasthan

Rajasthan was the home of the Rajputs, a group of warrior clans who controlled that part of northwest India for a thousand years. Their codes of conduct, chivalry, and honor were similar to those of the medieval European knights. Like the warring city-states of northern Italy, the Rajputs quarreled with each other when not fighting outsiders; thus, they never became united and were no match for the invading Mughals. But their bravery, honor, loyalty, and love of freedom have remained a legendary inspiration without parallel in the annals of most nations.

Rajput warriors seldom surrendered, regardless of the size of the invading army. When defeat was inevitable, the women and children committed suicide by marching into a funeral pyre in a ritual known as *jauhar*. The men put on saffron robes of celebration that were worn by them at weddings, and rode off to certain death. Time and time again in Rajput history, they chose the honor of death rather than surrender. It was not uncommon for tens of thousands of warriors to die this way in battle.

I met a Rajput of the *Kshatriya* (warrior) caste who told me that his father taught him only two things could stop a *Kshatriya* from succeeding: God and death. The noble Rajput legacy stirs my soul and always adds to the thrill of traveling in Rajasthan. The Rajputs' courage and valor have become part of the heritage of India.

Hawa Mahal (Palace of the Winds). Jaipur.

Jaipur

Jaipur is the capital city of the state of Rajasthan. It derived its name of the "pink city" from the pink-painted buildings which line the streets of its old walled city. It is not known when the tradition of painting the edifices pink began, but some say that it was initiated in 1876 to honor the visit of the Prince of Wales, who later became King Edward VII.

Jaipur's central landmark is the Hawa Mahal (Palace of the Winds). It is located in the old city and was built in 1799. The unusual five-story building is actually little more than a facade. It was built to enable ladies of the royal household to observe everyday life along the city streets without being seen. Carved stone lattice screens, which become more intricate with each successive story, cover every window.

From a rooftop vantage point at the local silver market, I watched an endless procession of people. Many of the women wore colorful Rajasthani clothing, and the men had on pastel turbans.

Many cows were present on the sidewalks, and occasionally one would walk into the streets, bringing an abrupt halt to the rush hour traffic. Usually someone would good-naturedly shoo the animal out of the way, but sometimes the sacred bovine received a not-so-propitious whack on the flanks with a long stick. Pedestrians shared the wide sidewalks with the cows, walking around them whenever one blocked their way. The coexistence of people and animals in the midst of a bustling city was a sight not to be seen in the West.

A street scene in the old city in the late afternoon. Jaipur.

A maze of small alleys intersected the broad avenues of the old city. The broad avenues and spacious bazaars were modeled after European cities. While wandering through them, I bought savory foods from several street vendors. Most Westerners that I met would not eat food sold on the streets, but it is usually safe to eat vegetarian foods provided they are obtained immediately upon being removed from the boiling oil.

The famous fortress-palace of Amber is located seven miles from Jaipur and was the ancient capital of the old state of Jaipur. Construction was begun in 1592 by the Rajput commander whom Akbar the Great, the famous Mughal Emperor of India, selected as the head of his armies.

Situated on a hillside and surrounded by walls, the citadel commands an imposing view of the neighboring mountains. To visit the maharaja's apartments on the upper level, I passed through the beautiful Hall of Victory, decorated with hundreds of lavishly glimmering wall panels.

On the ceiling, mirrors sparkled from the reflected sun. At the end of the open hall, there was an impressive view of the countryside, where protective walls traversed the barren mountains for great distances, resembling a smaller version of the Great Wall of China.

Amber Palace. Amber.

Stained glass windows of the throne room. The City Palace. Udaipur.

A wall painting of a royal elephant. The City Palace. Udaipur.

*Guards sitting in an interior courtyard.
The City Palace. Udaipur.*

The City Palace. Udaipur.

Udaipur

I thought Udaipur was the most beautiful city in India. Udaipur was founded in 1567 and is built around the lovely Pichola Lake. Palaces perched on rugged mountains form a picturesque backdrop. Most of Udaipur's houses and palaces are painted white, which reminded me of the splendor of Greek islands such as Mykonos. They present a handsome contrast to the blue lake and arid landscape.

The huge City Palace dominates the lake and is the largest palace complex in Rajasthan. It is a conglomeration of buildings, added over hundreds of years by various rulers, yet it retains a remarkable stylistic uniformity with its uniquely Indian gates, arches, towers, and cupolas. The Lake Palace, built in 1754, entirely covers a small island and has been converted into a luxury hotel.

I hired a motor rickshaw to tour the city, which enabled me to stay as long as I wished at several of its excellent museums and palaces. I was impressed by the grandeur of the City Palace, which is the residence of the line of maharajas who formerly ruled the princely state. With its brightly colored mosaics of peacocks, the favorite Rajasthani bird, it is one of India's most spectacular palaces.

The palace is known for its gracefully carved arches and 18th- and 19th-century Indian miniatures and paintings. The tiger hunting scenes from the Maharaja period of British colonialism depicted royal parties in regal howdahs riding on top of elephants.

Architectural detail of the City Palace. Udaipur.

Serpents protecting Parshavanatha.
Adinatha Jain temple. Ranakpur.

Ranakpur

Ranakpur is the largest and one of the most important Jain temples in India. The two-story structure, built in 1439, has many towers rising from its roof. Inside, 29 halls are supported by 1,944 pillars, no two alike. One of the intricately-carved pillars was purposely erected at an angle. The deliberate error symbolizes the imperfection of humankind.

Although Jainism was once an important religious movement in India, Jains now comprise less than 1 percent of India's population. The religion is contemporaneous with Buddhism and has similarities. It was founded in the 6th century B.C. by Mahavira (Great Spirit), the twenty-fourth and last of the Jain saints called *Tirthankaras*. The *Tirthankaras*, which means the ones who lead to the other shore, are also called *jinas* (victors or heroes), and their followers are called Jains, the sons of victors.

Jains conceive the universe to be infinite and believe that it was not created by a deity; yet, the religion is not atheistic. They believe the cosmos consists of imperishable particles that have always existed, some too small to be seen, all of which have souls.

The Jain belief in *ahimsa*, reverence for all life and the avoidance of injury to all living things, leads to the observance of strict vegetarianism. It also accounts for orthodox Jains wearing gauze masks over their faces to prevent swallowing or breathing on even the most minute micro-organisms. They also carry small brooms to sweep tiny insects from their paths as they walk.

Worshipers seated before an altar. Adinatha Jain temple. Ranakpur. 15th century.

Adinatha Jain temple. Ranakpur. 15th century.

A marble dome, Adinatha Jain temple. Ranakpur.

Rishabhanatha, also known as Adinatha, the first Jain saint. Adinatha Jain temple. Ranakpur.

A pujari (caretaker) making sandlewood paste. He wears a scarf over his nose to keep the ritual paste pure. Adinatha Jain temple. Ranakpur.

Meherangarh Fort. Jodhpur.

Jodhpur

Located on the edge of the Thar Desert, Jodhpur is dominated by a massive fort, standing atop a sheer rocky hill which rises abruptly in the middle of the city. The rocky cliffs provided an impenetrable barrier from several directions, making it the most formidable citadel in the "Land of the Kings." Entering the old part of the city was like stepping into a fairy tale. The men were wearing colorful turbans and had full moustaches, which curled at each end. The women were dressed in bright clothing, and they looked like images from travel posters.

A winding road led up to the Jodhpur fort from the city below. After passing through a series of gates, I noticed small handprints set into a wall. The handprints, or *sati* marks, belonged to Maharaja Man Singh's widows, who, in 1843, threw themselves upon his funeral pyre to be true to their vows. A garland of flowers had been placed around the handprints, commemorating the women's bravery and turning the wall into a shrine.

As a result of the Hindu matrimonial tradition of the wife totally surrendering her will to her husband's, a very strong bond of harmony often developed between them. At her husband's death, when the wife felt she could not live without him, she would throw herself upon his funeral pyre. The practice was known as *sati*, and in its very early days it was an uncoerced act of love and loyalty.

Though *sati* was originally optional, it was later carried out by force. If a woman refused to enter her husband's funeral pyre, she was often burned alive with him by his relatives to maintain the family's honor.

The British put an end to the custom by banning it. *Sati* had become a socially degrading act which tied a woman's destiny to that of her husband's, when her ultimate allegiance should be to God, not to man.

Historically, there were two grounds on which a woman in Rajasthan could take her own life: by *jauhar* or by *sati*. Because conquerors could force a marriage on his captive without her consent, Rajput women often chose to march into a funeral pyre to maintain their honor and to preserve the social custom of being married to only one man during their lifetime. This ritual known as *jauhar* was not a social evil, but had merit. The woman

The handprints (sati *marks*) of
Maharaja Man Singh's widows,
who threw themselves upon his
funeral pyre in 1843.
Meherangarh Fort. Jodhpur,
Rajasthan.

immolated herself for modesty. She was not forced into the action by anyone.

Sati, when performed voluntarily, was an act of devotion during that period. It showed the wife's unconditional love and loyalty to her husband. It was her ultimate gift—the giving of herself—even if it represented the limited understanding that existed during the Middle Ages.

Drastic measures, such as *sati* or the extreme flagellations performed by certain Catholic saints to overcome the ego, are no longer needed in this higher age. We now understand the science of Yoga and the purpose of ultimate fulfillment: to unite our souls with God. Today, greater spiritual perspective and yogic methods to obtain that union are available. Thus, it is an act of impiety for persons of our era to disparage the courageous acts of those women who gave their lives as their highest act of love.

After touring the lavish interiors of the maharaja's palace, I walked along the battlements of the once heavily-fortified walls. The view looking down on the old city was excellent. The houses were built so close together that the narrow streets were hardly discernible from that height. Most of the town's two-story buildings had flat roofs, which served as sleeping decks in the hot summer and were also used to dry red peppers. Crumbled old city walls could be seen in the distance, and beyond them were the rugged mountains and inhospitable countryside which was the beginning of the Thar desert. Perhaps a fourth of the houses were painted dark blue, which signified that the owners were *Brahmins*, members of the highest caste.

The Caste System

The idea of the caste system was originated by the great legislator Manu, who clearly perceived that humankind's natural evolution could be separated into four categories: *Brahmins*, those who have overcome the lower nature, are spiritually inspired, and if they are God-knowing, are able to teach and help liberate others;

A view of the old city. The blue houses signify that the owners are members of the Brahmin *caste. Jodhpur.*

Kshatriyas, those whose talents are administrative, executive, and protective (administrators and soldiers). They try to overcome bad habits and to control their senses; *Vaishyas*, those who are ambitious for worldly gain and interested in satisfaction of the senses. They have more creative abilities, such as businessmen, artists, and farmers; *Shudras*, those interested in satisfying their bodily needs and desires, and are best suited to offer service to society through physical labor.

People who perform the lowest menial tasks, such as cleaning toilets, sweeping streets, or working in the tanning industry, tasks that are considered unclean, are outside of the caste system and are known as the untouchables. Mahatma Gandhi did much to try to help the untouchables and gave them the name *Harijans* or "children of God," although today they prefer to be called the *Dalits*, which means oppressed.

The caste system, like dowries, originally had a good intent. Caste originally was not determined by one's birth, but by his or her natural tendencies. The ancient scripture the *Mahabharata* declares, "Neither birth nor sacraments nor study nor ancestry can decide whether a person is twice-born (a *Brahmin* or priest); character and conduct only can decide." In ancient India, ungenerous men of great wealth were assigned a low rank in the society. It is interesting to note that throughout India's long history, a large percentage of Hindu saints have come from the non-*Brahmin* castes.

A man wearing a Rajasthani turban. Jodhpur.

For thousands of years, the caste system traditionally provided the organizational basis for the Hindu society and determined the division of the social structure to which an Indian belonged. Many profound Indian thinkers credit the caste system with having preserved the purity of the Indian people over the millenniums. Serious evils resulted as stratification of the caste system gradually developed through the centuries as a result of the vested interests of the Brahmins. When movement was no longer allowed between castes, exploitation began.

The Constitution of India specifically abolishes untouchability, and its practice in any form is forbidden and is a punishable offense under the law. It also prohibits discrimination on grounds of religion, race, caste, sex, or place of birth. The Preamble to the Constitution resolves to secure justice, liberty, equality of status, and opportunity for all its citizens. Though the need to ameliorate the odious conditions of the untouchables had been recognized for a long time, it was only after independence that an effort was made on a national scale.

In modern India, caste and class are not interchangeable words. Much of the contemporary conflicts between castes have occurred in rural areas, where tensions result when the lower castes have become the upper class through economic gain. Although caste distinction still remains rigidly determined by birth, progress has been made since India's independence in 1947 in restoring the system to its original intent. Today, a *Shudra*, a member of the lowest caste, can be a government employee, a professor, or an officer in the military (the *Kshatriya* caste). The fact that a past president of modern India was from the lowest caste certainly offers hope for the future.

All nations recognize humankind's four natural divisions according to their abilities: laborers, businessmen, soldiers and administrators, and teachers and clergy. Those races and nations whose social customs discourage intermarriages between social classes practice certain aspects of the caste system.

After an overview of Jodhpur from the ramparts of the fort, I decided to have a closer look. The open markets in the old city were a photographer's dream. Several underfed cows with pronounced ribs wandered contentedly among mounds of produce, reflecting the enigma of their Hindu heritage.

An ascetic walking across the desert sands. Pushkar, Rajasthan.

The Hindu pilgrimage town of Pushkar.

Pushkar

I departed for Pushkar on a packed bus. Even the aisles were filled with people and their belongings. Though the Rajasthani men's bright red, orange, and pastel turbans gave a festive appearance to the crowded interior, I was glad when I finally arrived at my destination.

Located at the foot of a mountain on the edge of a desert, Pushkar is an important Hindu pilgrimage center, although it is better known in the West for its annual camel fair that attracts huge numbers of travelers from all over the world. The peaceful town is built around the sacred Pushkar Lake, said to have formed miraculously when Lord Brahma, the first part of the Hindu Trinity, dropped a lotus at that spot. Very close to the lake is Pushkar's most famous temple, said to be the only one in India dedicated to Brahma.

Having arrived after dark, I was totally unprepared for the magnificent view of this oasis, which greeted me the next morning from the roof of my hotel. Many stately white buildings and temples were built all around the lake, right up to the water's edge. Terraced stone stairs led down the gentle slope to the water, enabling bathers to approach the hallowed lake with ease. A few pilgrims were performing their morning rituals, while others were washing their clothes. The blurred images of the white edifices were reflected in the calm, azure water. The tranquil lake gave the town an appearance of a bygone era unspoiled by mechanization.

Climbing the steps to several small temples on the steep mountainsides offered a test of stamina to the pilgrims' devotion. A few green trees provided a stark contrast to the yellow sands of the desert, which stretched as far as I could see.

That night at dinner, I had a delicious vegetable dish served with *kulcha*, freshly baked bread filled with onions. The gourmet meal cost less than a dollar. On the way back to my hotel, I got rid of the *prasad* (sweets)

A man cooking sweets. Pushkar.

in my pocket that I had received at a temple earlier that day. A hungry cow in the narrow street accepted the offering, which had been rejected by two dogs whose haunt near a sweet stall had taught them to be more discriminating.

Since it was a pilgrimage center, Pushkar had many shops which sold delicious sweets. Small pieces of candy, wrapped in thin sheets of pure silver, were neatly stacked on counters in arrangements up to a foot high. The silver wrapping is eaten with the sweet, for in India, ingesting silver is thought to be good for one's health.

Men were cooking desserts in skillets over an open fire. Bowls containing milk, sugar, and other ingredients were sitting uncovered to cool, while flies congregated on the rims to sample the savory sweets. A few of the braver and greedier two-winged insects, not satisfied with a fly's portion, ventured into the center where they gorged themselves to death, becoming trapped as the contents thickened.

Early the next morning, I boarded a crowded bus which took me over the craggy mountain separating Pushkar from the nearby city of Ajmer. I had thoroughly enjoyed my visit and felt refreshed from my rest.

Sweets with thin, edible silver coverings. Pushkar.

A woman buying red peppers at an outdoor market. Ajmer.

Ajmer

Ajmer is built around a large lake at the base of barren hills. It is an interesting city with a long Muslim history. Akbar used to make annual pilgrimages there from Agra. One of the first contacts between the Mughals and the British occurred in Ajmer in 1616, when Jahangir met with Sir Thomas Roe. Today, Ajmer is a major pilgrimage site during the month of Ramadan, when Muslims observe a complete fast from sunrise to sunset.

One of India's most sacred sites for Muslims is the *dargah* (tomb) of Khwaja Moinuddin Chishti. The Sufi saint came to Ajmer in 1192 from Persia. For the Muslims of South Asia, the shrine is next in importance to

A flower stall near the dargah *(tomb) of a Sufi (Muslim) saint, Khwaja Moinuddin Chishti. Ajmer.*

Mekkah (Mecca). Every year on the anniversary of the saint's death, the tomb attracts hundreds of thousands of pilgrims. The shrine is revered by Hindus as well as Muslims.

Located outside the entrance gate, proprietors sat proudly at their flower stalls. They had arranged brightly colored blossoms so neatly in bins that from a distance, I thought they were sweets.

Jaisalmer

I left early the following morning by bus for the medieval walled city of Jaisalmer, located in the desert near India's western border with Pakistan.

Hundreds of years ago, Jaisalmer acquired great wealth from its strategic location on the camel caravan routes between India and Central Asia. Wealthy merchants built mansions called *havelis*, which were constructed from golden-yellow sandstone, the same material used to build the rest of the city. Jaisalmer gradually lost its hegemony as ships replaced camel caravans.

The devastating economic effects of World War II and Indian partition, which cut off trade routes through Pakistan, resulted in Jaisalmer's becoming nearly deserted. It was revived by its military importance after the 1965 and 1971 Indo-Pakistani wars. Since then, the increasing number of travelers who are attracted to this medieval city have given it an economic boost.

The medieval walled city of Jaisalmer.

The Jaisalmer fort was built in 1156 and sits on top of a sand hill 240 feet high. About one-fourth of the old city's inhabitants live within the confines of the fort's walls, which have a total of 99 bastions around its circumference.

Walking through the narrow streets of the old town, I came upon a series of houses which had religious folk art paintings on them. I visited an exquisitely-carved Jain temple that was over 500 years old. Around the inner walls were over a thousand stone figures, seated in the classical Jain pose. Round cosmology tablets and a large plaque with miniature figures were carved so intricately that the details looked more like Japanese ivory *netsukes* (toggles) than sandstone carvings.

The major tourist attraction around Jaisalmer is a camel safari. Having once had a sunstroke in Egypt while riding a horse across the desert from the Great Pyramid of Giza to the stepped pyramid of Saqqara, I thought it would be wise not to go.

I met a young English woman and her husband, both physicians who were living in New Zealand. Together with a Swiss man I had met on the bus trip to Jaisalmer, we rented a Land Rover for an excursion to some of the nearby attractions. We visited a cluster of old tombs near an oasis. Their open, graceful arches allowed a full view of the barren desert sand, which seemed a fitting background for the memorials and a reminder that no one escapes the eternal reaper, Death. While the four of us were discussing the poverty of Rajasthan, one of India's poorest states which was experiencing a drought, the doctor mentioned that when living in Africa with her parents, she had seen a famine.

She recounted a story of traveling with her family, when they were approached for food by some starving Africans. She commented that she was glad she did not have to make the decision of whether to give them their supply of rations. The experience obviously had a profound effect on her. I believe that her rigid insistence that giving money or food would make people beggars was her way of avoiding having to deal with a situation that revived unpleasant memories. She was not unique, as I have observed that many Westerners use their own mind-blocks to avoid feeling the emotional pain of others' suffering.

A Rajasthani woman.
Jaisalmer, Rajasthan.

I was brought up in a different cultural tradition from the British doctor. I, too, vividly recall an event from my childhood. Outside a movie theater in my hometown, we approached a handicapped man with a metal cup filled with pencils, sitting on the sidewalk. My grandfather, who was an immigrant from Lithuania, gave my brother and me money to give to him, with strict instructions not to accept a pencil, but at the beggar's insistence, we did. I will always remember my grandfather's scolding for our causing the man to have to buy more pencils.

Late that afternoon, we arrived at the sand dunes. I took off my shoes and enjoyed walking barefoot. That was my first experience with the peace of the desert, and I could understand its eternal allure for those seeking solitude.

As I sat on top of a dune, the pure white sand was bathed in a golden glow from the setting sun, now low on the horizon. Below me was a wind-formed crater, whose softly-lighted sand appeared as smooth as silk.

Just behind the crater was a sand pyramid whose dark and light sides could have been a symbol for duality. Zigzag furrows created a black-and-white pattern on the powdery surface. Nature's show of light and shadow was spectacular.

A puppet show. Jaisalmer.

The Thar Desert at sunset. Jaisalmer.

The carved marble interior of Vimal Vasahi Temple. Jain. Dilwara, Mt. Abu. A.D. 1032.

Mt. Abu

My travels next took me to Mt. Abu. The rugged mountains in that part of Rajasthan reminded me of Wales. At a rest stop in a small town during the long bus trip, many passengers bought buffalo milk that was being boiled over an open fire. The vendor skimmed a little cream from the surface of the steaming liquid and placed it in each glass. The hot drink of milk, sugar, and cream tasted delicious.

Located on a plateau at an elevation of over 3,600 feet, Mt. Abu is the only hill station in the state of Rajasthan. Besides serving as a mountain retreat during the scorching Indian summers, Mt. Abu is an important pilgrimage point for people of the Jain religion because of the intricately carved Dilwara Temples. The town is also a favorite spot for couples on their honeymoon. Since it was winter, the hill town was not crowded.

I took a bus tour to the famous Jain Dilwara Temples. The temples are among the finest examples of Jain architecture in India and were built during the late Medieval period, from 1032 to 1233. The delicacy of the interior of the earlier and more important Vimal Vasahi Temple takes marble carving to unsurpassed heights. The columns were connected by filigreed buttresses that reach to the ceiling. The inverted V-shaped architectural supports probably shifted some of the heavy weight from the marble domed ceiling to the columns, similar to the vaulting of a Roman aqueduct.

Surrounding the main temple is a courtyard that was made distinctive by 58 small cells once used by Jain ascetics. White marble porticoes marked the entrance to each small enclosure, which contain various marble statues of Jain saints.

After the half-day tour was completed, I climbed into the back of a crowded jeep that functioned as a mini-bus. Its fixed route from the Jain temple provided me with a quick and inexpensive ride to the *ashram* where I was staying. When I returned, the *sadhu* had prepared a delicious lunch for me consisting of *dahl* (lentils), potatoes, a vegetable dish I could not identify, rice, and *chapatis*. He gave me such huge servings that I could not eat it all.

Later that afternoon, while we were sitting outside in the sunshine, two cows walking by responded immediately when the *sadhu* called to them and enjoyed being fed my uneaten *chapatis*. His good nature was evident while feeding them, even as he pretended to be firm when he sent them away. He returned to his chair with a chuckle and a gleam in his eyes.

I noticed that the skin on his feet was splitting, presumably from exposure to the cold temperature, which covered the ground with frost that morning. He wore a sweater and a wool hat, but his lower body was covered only by a thin, cotton *lungi* (sarong). He washed the temple daily, and when he returned from his duties, I could tell his hands and feet were freezing from the way he warmed them around his small fire. I enjoyed being in his loving, peaceful presence and will always fondly remember my two days with the "gentle giant."

Dancing apsaras (heavenly nymphs) on marble pillars. Vimal Vasahi Temple. Dilwara, Mt. Abu. ca. 13th century.

I left Mt. Abu by bus to go to Ahmedabad, located in the neighboring state of Gujarat. Seated on one side of me was an Indian couple who were on their honeymoon. They were wearing blue jeans, which are considered chic for newlyweds to wear in rustic areas. The road was very bumpy, and since we were sitting over the rear wheels of the bus, we were bounced off our seats frequently. She took advantage of each occasion to utter a cute, soft shriek, much like a teenager, which always got her a hug or loving touch from her husband. Most Hindus do not display affection publicly, and except for children, that was the first time I had seen it done.

The courtyard of Vimal Vasashi Temple. Jain. Dilwara, Mt. Abu. A.D. 1032.

Schoolgirls, Church of the Immaculate Conception. Panaji (Panjim), Goa.

Chapter Five

The West

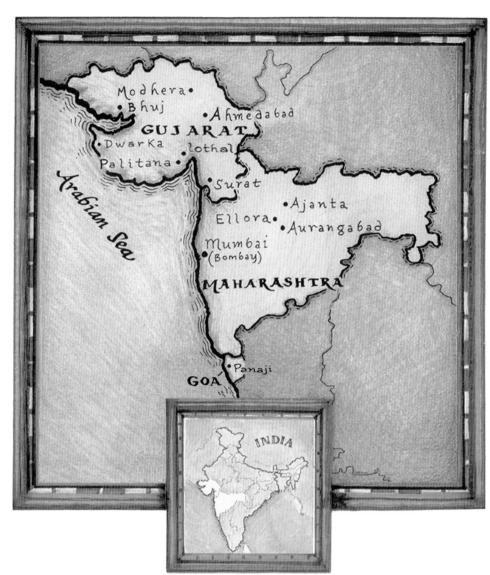

◁ *Opposite*
Detail of sculptures near the bottom
of a stepwell. Patan, Gujarat.

The West: Goa, Maharashtra, and Gujarat

Goa is well-known to foreigners for its superb white sandy beaches and crystal-clear turquoise water. For a discerning wayfarer, the small enclave's Portuguese heritage is also noteworthy, particularly its early Christian churches.

Mumbai (Bombay), the capital of Maharashtra, serves as an international gateway to India. Located a full day's journey northeast of the modern city are the world-famous Ajanta and Ellora caves. I found Ajanta to be the most interesting place that I visited in India.

Few tourists spend much time in the state of Gujarat, which is located between Maharashtra and Rajasthan. Yet I would consider the Jain mountaintop pilgrimage center of Palitana to be an exceptional place which should not be missed. It has over 850 temples, some almost 1,000 years old. It is a five-hour bus trip from Ahmedabad, the city where Mahatma Gandhi established the Sabarmati Ashram, his headquarters during the long struggle for India's independence from the British. I also enjoyed my visit to Dwarka, a picturesque seaside pilgrimage town, which was once the capital of Lord Krishna's kingdom.

The isolated westernmost part of Gujarat, known as the Kutch, has retained much of its tradition, and I was glad that I made the journey to its old walled city of Bhuj. Inside its richly decorated Swaminarayan Temple, I met an Indian resident whose daughter now lives in my hometown of Columbus, Georgia. Karma!

A woman dressed in traditional clothing, selling Indian textiles. Anjuna Beach, Goa.

Goa: Portuguese Splendor of the Past

The Portuguese arrived in Goa in 1510. With its natural harbors and wide rivers, Goa was an ideal location for the seafaring Portuguese who were intent on controlling the spice route across the Indian Ocean and were also eager to spread Christianity. Jesuit missionaries, led by St. Francis Xavier, arrived in Goa in 1542.

Goa's golden age came when the Portuguese eventually took control of the trade routes from the Turks. This enabled the Portuguese to make fortunes from the spice trade, and Goa became the seat of the Portuguese Empire of the East that included Timor, Macau, and East African port cities.

With the exception of a brief occupation by the British during the Napoleonic Wars in Europe, the Portuguese maintained their hegemony over Goa for 450 years until 1961 when the province was taken by force, and Goa became the 25th state of India. Today's population of Goa is predominantly Christian, reflecting its 16th-century conquest by the Portuguese.

Goa still maintains its distinctively Portuguese appearance and slow-paced life. I had gone to Goa to escape the commotion of Indian life, so the soft, warm sand and palm-fringed beaches that stretch for miles and miles were inviting.

St. Francis Xavier holding a cross. Polychrome wood. Basalica of Bom Jesus. Old Goa, Goa. 1594–1605.

Church of St. Francis of Assisi. Old Goa, Goa. 1661.

The main altar, dedicated to St. Catherine of Alexandria. Se Cathedral, Old Goa. Completed in 1652.

Old Goa

Located about six miles from the old Portuguese town of Panaji (Panjim), the state capital, is the city of Old Goa. During the 16th century, the wealthy Portuguese city grew rapidly, eventually rivaling Lisbon. Large churches, monasteries, and convents were built by the religious orders that came to Goa under royal mandate. The interiors of some of the churches are as lavish as those of Spain and Portugal. Old Goa's splendor did not last long, for at the end of the 16th century, Portugal's supremacy on the seas was replaced by the English, Dutch, and French.

As I approached the city by bus, a thrill went through my body when I caught my first glimpse of the huge white churches extending through the canopy of the lush foliage. It was as if I were entering another era.

The largest church at Old Goa is the Se Cathedral. The Portuguese-Gothic structure was begun in 1562 and took more than 55 years to build. Completing the altars took an additional 45 years.

To me, Goa's most interesting church was the Church of St. Francis of Assisi. Built on the site of an earlier chapel constructed by eight Franciscan friars who arrived in 1517, the current building dates to 1661. Two turrets give the church a fortress-like appearance. In addition to the gilded carved woodwork, old murals depict scenes from the life of St. Francis.

The Basilica of Bom Jesus contains the tomb of Goa's patron saint, St. Francis Xavier. He arrived in Goa in 1542 to spread Christianity along the Malabar and Coromandel coasts. His missionary zeal took him to Indonesia, Japan, and an island off the coast of China, where he died at age 46. His body evidently remained in a state of incorruptibility for perhaps 100 years, and he was canonized in 1622. His glass coffin is displayed for public view every 10 years.

Mumbai (Bombay), Maharashtra

The Gateway of India, the Taj Intercontinental, and the Taj Mahal Hotel. Mumbai (Bombay).

Mumbai (Bombay)

Mumbai, India's largest city and financial capital, is one of the five largest cities in the world. It was ceded to Portugal in the 16th century before the British took control. By the early 18th century, it had become the British East India Company's headquarters for trade on the west coast of India.

Mumbai has retained its title of "The Gateway of India" and is India's most cosmopolitan city. It has a modern stock exchange in which large numbers of middle-class families buy shares. Mumbai's movie industry is the largest in the world. It's Bollywood fame has attracted the attention of Hollywood.

Overlooking the city from the top of Malabar Hill are the formal Hanging Gardens. Located next to the gardens, but carefully concealed from view, are the Parsi Towers of Silence. The Parsis are followers of Zoroastrianism, one of the oldest religions in the world. The religion was founded in Persia by the prophet Zarathustra (Zoroaster). Because Parsis believe in the purity of the elements (earth, water, fire, air) and do not wish to pollute them, they do not cremate or bury their dead. Instead, the corpses are placed within the Towers of Silence, where vultures do the rest.

Fleeing persecution in Persia, the Parsis migrated to Gujarat and moved to Mumbai in large numbers in the late 17th century. Though the number of Parsis in India is drastically diminishing, because of their philanthropy and success in commerce and industry, their influence far exceeds their numbers.

During my first visit to Mumbai, I stayed with an Indian family. One day, they invited me to accompany them to the Mahalakshmi Temple. I was delighted to go, of course.

Mahalakshmi Temple, Mumbai's oldest temple, sits majestically on a hill overlooking the Arabian Sea. It is dedicated to Lakshmi, the goddess of wealth, an appropriate patron deity for this thriving city of commerce.

Before entering Hindu temples and homes, a person removes his shoes. Unlike Western churches and synagogues, there are no pews inside on which to sit. The interior is an open space, except for an altar at the rear of the temple. Lengthy services and sermons have no function here. Prayer books are not necessary to offer the untutored chords of one's heart. Spontaneity of devotion requires no formal structuring.

With a basket of flowers and sweets as an offering from all of us, we made our way forward, passing through a constant stream of pilgrims returning from the altar. Two Hindu priests were sitting on the altar in front of an impressive statue of Lakshmi, covered with garlands of flowers. I stood in front of one of the seated priests, not knowing what to do. One of our group who was standing behind me observed my predicament and pushed my arms toward the priests. One of them took the basket from me. Then, placing the fingers and palms of both

hands together in a ritual gesture of respect, we *pranamed* to the image of
Goddess Lakshmi.

The ritual conducted by the priest was ingenious. While intoning a prayer,
he placed the offering at Lakshmi's feet. Then, he picked up an offering that
had already been accepted and blessed by the goddess, and distributed it to
the pilgrims. The eagerly sought sweets, known as *prasad*, are believed to be
divinely blessed. For those who remained at the altar, another priest placed a
mark on the spiritual eye at their forehead.

Staying in an Indian home enabled me to gain insight into the Indian culture.
The amount of affection Seema and her two sisters gave to her 11-month-old
son, Karan, touched my heart. Nandini, the middle sister, referred to herself
as his second mother, and indeed she was. When I spoke to Seema about how
much time she spent playing with her son, she replied, "We in India do not
have much materially to give our children, so we make up for it by giving a
lot of love." My personal feelings about the importance of parental love were

*A flower stall. Mahalakshmi Temple.
Mumbai (Bombay).*

echoed by Mother Teresa when she told an American couple, "I have seen the starving [on the streets of Kolkata],
but in your country, I have seen an even greater hunger. That is the hunger to be loved. No place in all of my
travels have I seen such loneliness as I have seen in the poverty of affluence in America."

While walking in the neighborhood one day, I passed a two-story building with a low fence around it, where
a large group of well-dressed women were eagerly waiting. The event looked promising, so I decided to wait
and see what developed. In a short time, the doors opened, and young schoolboys came running out. They were
dressed in uniforms of tan shirts and shorts, like Boy Scouts. A few moments later, the girls came out, which
led me to believe that boys and girls were taught in separate classes, according to the custom of ancient Hindu
tradition. The mothers called and waved to their children and affectionately hugged and greeted them. It was
hard for me to believe that the children received such a warm welcome every day after school. In the West, one
does not see such display of emotion on a daily basis, and it was quite a contrast to Western carpools. It was
the type of greeting I would have received after returning home from a two-month summer camp.

A children's ride. Juhu Beach. Mumbai (Bombay).

Buddhist caves. Ajanta.

Ajanta and Ellora Caves

I boarded a local bus to Ajanta from the train station at Jalgaon. Many school-children were visiting the caves that day. They were friendly and inquisitive, and every few minutes one of them asked me, "What country are you from?" Because few American tourists go to Ajanta, most did not guess that I was from the United States.

Several Indian tourists whom I met gave me their addresses and extended invitations for me to visit them. School-children sang an Indian song for me, and a young girl did a "disco" dance. With the least encouragement, they would grin and speak to me in English. The friendliness of the children and adults was almost as memorable as the famous caves.

The 29 caves at Ajanta are carved into a steep, horseshoe-shaped gorge, which was formed by a small river flowing at its base. The Buddhist caves at Ajanta predate those of Ellora and contain some of the oldest surviving examples of Indian paintings. The caves were carved from the 2nd century B.C. to the 7th century A.D., when Buddhism was waning in India. Once abandoned, the rock-cut sanctuaries became overgrown and were lost. They were not rediscovered until 1817, when a British hunting party in quest of tigers stumbled upon them, and the splendor of the Ajanta Caves was known to the world.

A wide walkway along the ravine's wall makes the caves easily accessible. Many of them have large columns with intricately carved capitals, giving an illusion that they are supporting the massive sanctuaries. The columns were actually not needed architecturally, since all the caves were hollowed out from rocks.

The caves originally served as monasteries (*viharas*), but by the 5th century A.D., their purpose was extended to include shrines for worship (*chaityas*). I was more inspired by the earlier Hinayana Buddhist caves than I was by the later and more elaborate Mahayana ones. Most of the realistic paintings portrayed the various incarnations of the Buddha and were depicted in contemporary settings of the artists' world. A variety of muted colors gave the frescoes a venerable look.

Elaborately carved porches covered with Buddha images were attached to the outer facade of some caves. They made impressive entrances to the sanctuaries, which were adorned with graceful columns and frescoes. The ceilings of a few of them emulated in stone the vaulted arches of timber, much like the ceilings of early Gothic cathedrals. A large image of the Buddha peered out from a darkened shrine room. The superb sculptures at Ajanta and Ellora compare favorably to marble carvings of the Greco-Roman period.

A large seated Buddha and other statuary. Ajanta Caves.

Buddhas carved in bold relief. Ajanta Caves.

A wall painting of Princess Arundati on a swing. Cave 2. Ajanta. Gupta dynasty, 5th–6th century A.D.

Buddhist sculpture. Cave 2.
Ajanta, Maharashtra.
5th–6th century A.D.

Carved into an escarpment of volcanic stone that rises above the plains of the northern Deccan plateau are the world-renowned Ellora Caves near Aurangabad. They were once an old pilgrimage center for the Buddhists, Hindus, and Jains. While Ajanta is known for its paintings, Ellora is one of the greatest of all Indian sites for sculpture. The 29 caves at Ajanta are all Buddhist, while at Ellora, 12 caves are Buddhist, 17 are Hindu, and 5 are Jain. It is thought that the builders of Ajanta moved to Ellora when construction at the earlier site abruptly halted around the 7th century.

The masterpiece and central attraction at Ellora is the Kailasanatha Temple which rises almost 100 feet above the carved courtyard floor. Like the elaborate cave-temples at Ajanta, meticulous advance planning of the entire project was essential, because unlike conventional architecture, success depended on what was removed rather than what was constructed. The huge temple covers twice the area of the Parthenon in Athens and is almost twice as high.

◁ *Opposite*
A wall painting of the Bodhisattva *Padmapani holding a lotus. Cave 1. Ajanta, Maharashtra. Gupta dynasty, late 5th century A.D.*

The Buddha preaching the Law. Carved on a stupa. *Cave 10. Ellora. ca. A.D. 700–750.*

A carved stone window with the Tree of Life motif. Sidi Saiyad's Mosque. Ahmedabad.

Opposite▷
A Muslim reading the Qur'an in the early morning. Jama Masjid (mosque). Ahmedabad, Gujarat. 1424.

Ahmedabad

Ahmedabad is one of India's major industrial cities and is the largest city in Gujarat. Though it is better known for its textile industry, it has some of the finest examples of Islamic architecture in India.

Though the city was noisy and polluted, I liked it. The streets were narrow and crowded with pedestrians and all kinds of vehicles. It seemed to me that the street's center line served as nothing more than a median, delineating equal distance on either side. Drivers had little respect for its presence. The main rule for driving in India is "might makes right." Trucks forced cars off the road, cars forced three-wheeled motor rickshaws and motor scooters off the road, and pedestrians had to fend for themselves.

Ahmedabad can be very hot in the summer. On one of my visits, the temperature reached 119 degrees Fahrenheit. It was the hottest weather I had ever encountered.

I visited a small village near Ahmedabad, where many of the inhabitants lived a simple, communal life. While engaged in a discussion, a man with very little education, whom Westerners would consider uninformed, asked me to tell Americans: "If they would do their work in a spirit of service to God, it would help them to loosen the grip of the ego."

Modhera

About 70 miles northwest of Ahmedabad is the Sun Temple of Modhera. I was eager to visit the temple because of a strange occurrence in Goa. While eating breakfast near a beach one morning in an almost empty restaurant, an Indian man approached my table. Placing in front of me a magazine that was opened to color photographs of a temple located about a thousand miles away in Gujarat, he said, "You should go there." My body immediately tingled as if in confirmation of his directive. Writing down the name and location of the temple, I put the encounter in the back of my mind.

Modhera was the temple pictured in the magazine which was thrust upon me in Goa. My host, Rakesh, and the family's young houseboy were happy to accompany me on the journey. Upon entering the sacred shrine room, once dedicated to the Sun God Surya, I felt peaceful vibrations somehow connected to the ruined temple's past. It was as if the peaceful currents flowed directly into my physical body. To be sure I was not imagining it, I would go outside, then return to the sacred precinct for comparison. Of the hundreds of temples I visited in India, this was the site where I was most aware of the spiritual vibrations. Why the man in Goa approached me with the magazine article on Modhera remains one of the enigmas of my life.

A partial view of the Jain temples on top of the sacred hill of Shatrunjaya. Palitana.

Palitana

In a downtown office building in Ahmedabad, I saw a picture which caught my fancy. When I inquired about it, I was told that those were *derasars* (Jain temples) on top of the holy mountain at Palitana in southwest Gujarat. I knew that I would go there, and early the following morning, I went to the bus station.

Indian bus stations are often chaotic. Sometimes buses leave from designated platforms, but other times, they just stop in a general area and people push and shove to get aboard. If the bus does not leave from a designated bay, it can be very confusing for a foreigner. In all of my travels throughout India, someone always came forward whenever I needed help. In this instance, a young boy selling newspapers showed me my bus when it arrived. He took me by the hand sweetly, and escorted me inside the bus.

The top of the mountain at Palitana is known as Shatrunjaya, the Place of Victory, and is one of the holiest Jain pilgrimage sites. Over a period of 900 years, more than 860 temples have been constructed atop this peak, which rises steeply to a height of 7,288 feet. The earliest temples were built during the 11th century, but they were destroyed in the 14th and 15th centuries by the Muslims, who, with a few exceptions were not known for their religious tolerance. The existing temples date from the 1500s to the present.

I engaged a horse cart in front of my hotel to take me to the base of the famous mountain that was a little over a mile away. Those whose age or health did not permit the physical exertion required to ascend the hundreds of steps to the summit could hire a *doli* (swing chair), which was supported on the

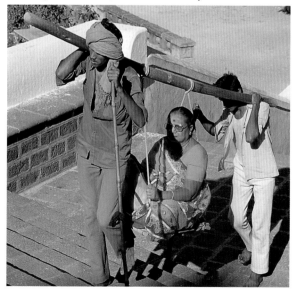

Jain woman being carried up mountain in doli. *Palitana.*

shoulders of two porters. The cost of being carried up the steep incline was partially determined by the weight of the rider. Because of Jain respect for all life, no leather, including shoes and watchbands, may be worn on the sacred mountain.

A caretaker of a Jain temple carrying fruits for offerings. Shatrunjaya, Palitana.

As I reached the top of the mountain, I appreciated the Herculean effort that must have gone into transporting the building materials for the temples. High walls gave the hilltop the appearance of a fortress. Inside the sacred precinct, temples were grouped into nine separate compounds, or *tuks*, each with a central temple surrounded by many minor ones. The narrow streets reminded me of the medieval walled cities of Europe. From the top of the walls, there was a panoramic view of the Gulf of Cambay. The sparkling azure water provided a contrast to the parched, rugged countryside that had been experiencing a drought for many years.

Like the Jain temples at Mt. Abu, the temples at Palitana had some of the most intricately carved interiors I had ever seen. The filigree carvings gave credence to the traditional story that the sculptors did not carve the marble with tools, but worked it with abrasive cords and were paid at the end of each day according to the size of the pile of marble dust they had accumulated!

Overhead, massive elaborate decorations on the ceiling transformed marble into intricate geometric designs of lace, which hung downward like stalactic snowflakes clustered together to form a canopy.

As sunset approached, I headed towards the main gate because no one, not even a priest, was allowed to remain on the mountain after dusk. Early the following morning, I departed for Ahmedabad.

Jain temples at one of the nine tuks *(compounds) at Shatrunjaya. Palitana.*

A yajna *ceremony. Priest offering grains into a sacred fire, symbolizing the burning of one's bad Karma in the fires of wisdom. The nuns are wearing red saris. Swaminarayan Temple. Bhuj, Gujarat.*

Gujarat's Indus Valley Civilization

The Indus Valley civilization (2800 B.C.–1800 B.C.) is one of the oldest urban civilizations in the world. It developed along the Indus River in the northwest Indian subcontinent in present-day Pakistan. The two most well-known centers that have been excavated were at Harappa and Mohenjo-daro.

Lothal, which is located in Gujarat about 50 miles southwest of Ahmedabad, was an important port city of the Indus Valley civilization. Discovery of seals at Lothal, about 450 miles southeast of Mohenjo-daro, would suggest that the Indus civilization from this part of the Indian subcontinent traded with the ancient civilizations of Mesopotamia, Egypt, and Persia.

Recent scientific evidence suggests that an ancient civilization indigenous to India predates the Indus Valley civilization. References to the ancient Saraswati River in the Rig Veda, the oldest Hindu scripture, were believed to be a myth by the British. Recently, French satellite imaging, supported by limited excavations, has revealed the course of the ancient Saraswati River, giving credibility to the claim of India's ancient culture.

A team of Indian marine archaeologists has discovered a huge underwater city off the coast of Gujarat. Preliminary carbon datings indicate the submerged city predates the Indus Valley civilization.

Dwarka

The sacred, picturesque town of Dwarka overlooks the Arabian Sea on the western tip of Gujarat. Archaeological excavations show that present-day Dwarka is the sixth city on that site, the earlier five having been submerged in the sea. Like the discovery of ancient Troy on the western coast of Turkey by Heinrich

Moon behind the Dwarkanath Temple at sunrise. Dwarkanath is a title of Lord Krishna. Dwarka, Gujarat.

A painting of Lord Krishna as a charioteer at the historic battle of Kurukshetra, counseling Prince Arjuna: "He who perceives Me everywhere and beholds everything in Me, never loses sight of Me, nor do I ever lose sight of him." —Bhagavan Krishna, Bhagavad Gita VI:30

Schliemann, Dwarka's antecedents played an important role in ancient history, and is closely associated with the legend of Krishna. It was once the capital of Lord Krishna's kingdom. It is one of the four most holy Hindu pilgrimage sites.

Surat, Gujarat

Surat, the second-largest city in the state of Gujarat, is about 150 miles north of Mumbai (Bombay). I was going there to visit Ajay and Jayshree, medical doctors whom I had met the previous year in California. They were expecting me, and Ajay picked me up at the train station in his car. After having been on a crowded train, I was happy to be traveling comfortably again!

After a delicious lunch, they acquainted me with various aspects of Indian life. Jayshree explained that the child is next in importance to God, and until the child is four or five years old, the parents make sacrifices and stay at home as much as possible. It is incomprehensible to most Indians how so many American mothers leave their young children so frequently.

While Ajay was visiting the United States, there had been a plane crash, and only one child survived. Ajay was amazed at the statement of the grandparent, who had not yet decided the "fate" of the boy. Most Hindu grandparents, regardless of their circumstances, would have adopted that child and raised him as their own.

The following day, one of Ajay's best friends had lunch with us. I liked him immediately. Dr. Patel explained to me that there is no formality in Indian friendships, and that the expression of "thank-you" is a phrase which leads to insincerity and perfunctory habit. No words of thanks are necessary, since the person is doing it because it is his or her *dharma* (duty). He said that it is okay to express an occasional thank you, but it is the warmth of the eyes and heart that reveal true feelings, making speech unnecessary. He added, "Words are meaningless without actions. We don't say 'I love you.' We just show it."

Gujarat

The Sun Temple. Modhera. A.D. 1026–27.

Homes in Gujarat have a distinctive feature that sets them apart from the rest of India: most of them have large swings inside. Because one of my earliest and happiest memories from childhood is swinging in a glider on our front porch with my parents and older brother, I never miss an opportunity to sit on a swing. When my preference became known, my hosts would get up from the swing to make room for me. Dr. Patel would often sit next to me on his swing, and we both enjoyed seeing how high we could go in his parlor.

A few days later, Dr. Patel invited me to accompany him on a trip to visit his parents, who lived in a small village several hundred miles north. We arrived at his parents' home in time for dinner. Since the "guest is God" in India, it was always a culinary delight for me to dine in an Indian home. I was served food until I had to admantly refuse it being placed on my plate.

Later that evening, Dr. Patel took me to the home of his good friend, who was the local Sanskrit teacher. The place was pitch dark when we arrived, but after we knocked, someone opened the door and led us up to a loft. A small light was turned on for us, and we quickly took a seat among the many children who had come to see the weekly television episode of the religious epic, the *Mahabharata*.

When the program was over, everyone left without speaking a word. I wondered if they were consciously practicing silence, a precursor of peace. They had been watching one of the few television sets in the village. It seemed that the entire nation came to a halt every Friday evening, when people watched the exciting dramatization of the ancient Hindu scripture. I later learned that more people watched this than any other program ever shown on Indian television. This is not surprising, considering the spiritual nature of the Hindu people.

Dr. Patel informed me one morning that we were going to visit his mother's family, who lived in a nearby village. Upon entering their house, we were offered the customary glass of water, but I was afraid to drink it for fear of contracting amoebic dysentery. Unlike previous situations when I refused, this time my conscience silently broadcast a loud and clear message that I should accept the water. Before drinking it, I prayed to God from the depth of my soul: "Lord, you know that I am drinking this water against my better judgment in order to not hurt these people's feelings, so please protect me!" Instantly, a strange sensation came over me, and I knew my prayer had been answered. From that moment onward, I drank tap water, water from the holy Ganges River, and water from various other sources with no adverse consequences. I truly believe that because of my deep love for Indians and my desire to have them know that their simple hospitality was sufficient for an American, I received a special dispensation from God. Later in America, I met an Indian doctor who was amazed to learn that I drank the water and ate any food I wanted. He said that even he could not do that without getting sick and explained scientifically how my faith had increased my stomach's secretion of hydrochloric acid, which killed germs and prevented me from becoming ill!

Later, we were invited to sit down on the floor for lunch, but Dr. Patel's mother's family did not eat with us as I had expected them to. Instead, they were our servers! After we finished our multiple-course dinner, they sat down and ate their meal. When we were preparing to leave, the family offered money to Dr. Patel's father, which is the custom when the husband visits his wife's family. He did not want to accept it, but finally, he took some token amount to satisfy them.

On my last day, Dr. Patel took me to a nearby village to meet a yogi. He lived in a small white-washed house with a faded religious painting on the front. For 14 years, he had not left his small compound, which he had made into a temple. He depended entirely on contributions and food that villagers left for him. Since he spoke no English, Dr. Patel served as an interpreter.

I was concerned when the yogi said that I had made a mistake in coming to India. Upon further questioning, he said that I could not find what I was looking for there. Like a swami we had met a few days previously, he was telling me that God was inside. He would not answer my questions directly and often responded that God manifests through everything, and that I should see and serve God in all.

The yogi said that we should always act from our heart, as devotion is necessary to open that center of feeling. He stated that marriage was the greatest delusion if it is not based on spiritual principles, and ties us to the physical world, separating us from God. He commented that it was good that I had never married, and that I should just serve God.

He was very particular about performing his spiritual duties at specific times, possibly to establish regular habits. In response to a question about healing the body, he said that a lady who had recently come to him with an incurable medical disease had gotten well after he gave her something to take.[1] He mentioned that someone else who visited him had a similar experience. Thanking him for his advice and leaving a donation inside his shrine, we knelt respectfully before him and departed with his blessings.

A yogi sitting in front of a painting depicting the prelude to creation, with Vishnu reclining on the cosmic serpent Ananta on the waters of Nara. His consort Lakshmi is massaging his feet. Gujarat.

A bride at her wedding reception. Indore, Madhya Pradesh.

A groom approaching his wedding reception on horseback in the Hindu tradition. New Delhi.

Marriage

In most Indian families, marriages are still arranged, although today, the children usually have a say in the selection process. The custom of not seeing one's spouse until the arrival at the marriage ceremony is a thing of the past. The potential marriage partners meet and talk with one another in the presence of their families to see if they satisfy each other's physical requirements and to determine if they are compatible. If both families agree after that first stage, then their horoscopes are exchanged and given to astrologers to ascertain that they are well-matched.

Westerners who are unfamiliar with Hindu culture cannot understand how arranged marriages are more successful than the Western process of choosing one's own mate. But they are. Hindu marriages are based on the principles of establishing friendship first, which forms a basis for a permanent relationship, and then developing love for each other. Currently in the West, there is such a high divorce rate. Could it be because the selection of one's mate usually is based on short-term emotional considerations and sex appeal, with neither party seeking the advice of his or her parents or minister? Divorces, until recently, were rare in Hindu marriages, and there is a saying: "To separate the marriage is to displease God." An Indian woman told me, "No matter what happens, we always think of giving marriage a chance."

A doctor I met on a train commented, "Hindu husbands and wives have arguments, but there are limits beyond which we do not go." Another Hindu traveler I met explained, "Indian women do not go to health spas to keep their figures trim like Western women, and after having babies, they often get plump. Yet we would never think of looking elsewhere." I now had the answer to my oft-pondered question of what Hindu men had done to deserve possibly the most loyal, devoted wives in the world. The answer: the Hindu husband's love, although often not shown outwardly, is reflected in his purity. Traditional Hindu values are breaking down rapidly, however, with the onslaught of Indian desire for Western technology and materialism.

Hindu women have an inner power and serenity that is seldom seen in the battle of the sexes in the West. Men may think that they run India, but the country's greatness actually comes from her women. They are the devotional ones who hold the marriage, family, and heterogeneous country together.

A brief story will illustrate the above point. On my return trip to America, I began a conversation with an Indian flight attendant. The young Hindu lady, who was living in Hong Kong, appeared "liberated" in a Western sense. When I asked her if she would be willing to subordinate her career and ego for the higher cause of marriage, she replied without hesitation, "Of course. What do you think makes us such good wives?"

I learned about the lifelong commitment a Hindu woman takes into a relationship in a most unexpected way. When visiting Indian friends in Central India, a 15-year-old girl asked if I could get her a penpal in America. When I was preparing to leave a week later, she had not returned, so I sent for her. As she handed me her address, she confided that the reason she had not come back was because she was not sure that she could commit to writing to someone for the rest of her life!

Perhaps one of the reasons that marriages are so unsuccessful in the world today is that most couples do not understand the principles on which to base a spiritual marriage. The famous yogi and world teacher Paramahansa Yogananda, author of *Autobiography of a Yogi*, one of the ten all-time best-selling autobiographies, has some cogent comments on the spiritual purposes of marriage. Yogananda explains that in man, reason is predominant,

A wedding ceremony. The knot tied between the groom's shawl and the bride's sari symbolizes unity between the couple and their families. Indore, Madhya Pradesh.

and in woman, feeling is the uppermost characteristic. Through marriage, man brings out the hidden reason in woman, and woman brings out the hidden feeling in man. All men can appreciate the saying which testifies to woman's emotional nature: "Woman convinced against her will is of the same opinion still!" Man is just as one-sided and acts too much from the intellect and not enough from his heart, as all women know. Through a spiritual marriage, each helps to balance the other's temperament.

By displaying love, friendship, consideration, respect, and other noble qualities for each other, the two souls merge into perfect harmony. But perfect harmony is not the goal of marriage, just as it is not the goal of one wave blown by the wind of delusion to merge with another wave. The goal is for both waves to dissolve back into the sea. Once husband

Groom and his sister arriving for his wedding. Gujarat.

and wife become one with each other, their united hearts are offered to God and merged back into the "ocean of Spirit." Spiritual marriage, when properly understood, becomes a beautiful (but often difficult!) path to God.

When traveling by train one day, I met an Indian who asked me if I thought I would ever marry. I answered, "Yes, if I ever met someone with whom I had soul unity." Looking at me with a smile, he replied, "Soul unity comes through many years of marriage."

Marriage is not a prerequisite for attaining balance between feeling and reason if an individual experiences a human relationship of pure love or friendship. But unconditional love must be perfected first on the physical plane before divine love can be achieved on the spiritual plane. If one cannot conquer human hearts, one will never win the heart of God.

Dowries

While dowries are much abused by the groom's family, one should remember that the custom originated to ensure a daughter gets a fair portion of her father's wealth. Most educated women in India today refuse to marry a man if he or his family demands a dowry. There are also numerous societies which oppose dowries and promote its abolition. It is primarily in rural areas and among less educated subcastes where the custom still prevails.

Though the Dowry Prohibition Act of 1961 clearly abolishes dowries, the bride's family often agrees to pay one. The oppressive dowry does not end with the wedding. The family of the bride is expected to continually provide nice gifts to the groom on special occasions or when the groom visits the family. Dowries can even ruin a family financially, depending on the ambitions that the bride's family has for their daughter. Sensational newspapers are filled with accounts of cruelties, beatings, and even murders of women by husbands who thought their dowries were insufficient. While it is often difficult to prove that a dowry is demanded, when conclusive evidence is available, a jail sentence is usually served. Exceptions are made for the state of Jammu and Kashmir and does not include certain Muslim marriage practices, which are regulated by their own religious laws.

Not all of India is patriarchal. In some regions of the state of Kerala in South India, the families are matriarchal. Women are the decision makers and play a dominant role. I was told that all over India, the maternal uncle often plays a key role in Hindu families.

In the families that I stayed with, women had the same status as women have in the West. Without exception, the husbands helped clear the dishes from the table after the meals and often performed other kitchen chores.

Like most abuses in India's ancient traditions, the dowry custom is changing for the better. With increasing numbers of women entering the workforce, eventually the forced dowry tradition will become outmoded.

The Shore Temple at sunset. Mamallapuram (Mahabalipuram), Tamil Nabu. Pallava dynasty, early 8th century A.D.

Chapter Six

The South

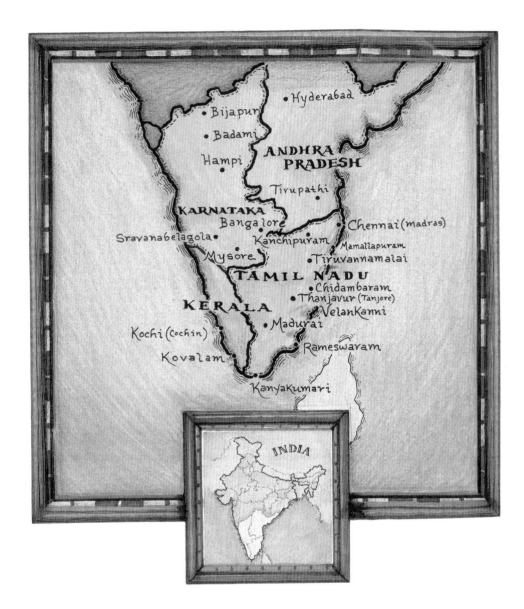

◁ *Opposite*
The ruins of the Chalukyan
capital. Badami, Karnataka.
Mid-6th to mid-8th century.

The South: Andhra Pradesh, Karnataka, Kerala, and Tamil Nadu

The extreme south of India was never conquered by the early Muslim invaders. Thus, its culture is discernibly different from that of the North. Most of the restaurants are vegetarian, meat having been introduced into northern diets by the Muslims. Much of the food was cooked with too many hot peppers for me to eat. The hot spices are meant to promote perspiration, which has a cooling effect on the body in that hot climate. In many restaurants in South India, dishwashing is kept to a minimum. My lunch and dinner were served on a banana leaf. The diner pours a little water on to it to wash the surface, and the excess is poured on the floor.

The best-known city in Andhra Pradesh is its capital of Hyderabad. The state has an interesting array of Muslim, Buddhist, and Hindu sites, including the holy mountain of Tirumala, accessible from Chennai (Madras).

Bangalore and Mysore are cosmopolitan cities in the state of Karnataka. The state's magnificent Hoysala temples and the archaeological sites of Hampi and Badami are worth visiting, as are the colossal temples in the southernmost state of Tamil Nadu located at Kanchipuram, Chidambaram, and Madurai to mention a few.

Kerala, located on the western seaboard fronting the Arabian Sea, is a quiet, rural area where life has a slow pace. It was as if the modern world had not yet penetrated the secluded hamlets of that state.

Andhra Pradesh

Andhra Pradesh is the biggest and most populous state in the south of India. It stretches over 750 miles along the east coast of India, from Orissa in the north to the southernmost state of Tamil Nadu. Its large land mass extends far inland. The history of eastern Andhra Pradesh dates back to King Ashoka in the 3rd century B.C. An ancient Buddhist site at Amaravathi, near the city of Vijayawada, has a *stupa* larger than the one at Sanchi. The Hindu temple on top of the holy mountain at Tirupathi is one of the most important pilgrimage places in India.

The region was dominated at various times by the Pallavas from Tamil Nadu, the Chalukyas from Karnataka, and the Cholas. The mid-16th century witnessed the rise of the Muslim Qutub Shahi Dynasty, a line of Muslim rulers who had ruled the mainly-Hindu population of the surrounding southern Deccan since the 14th century. Their large royal tombs still grace the landscape. The modern state was created in 1956 from a Telegu-speaking region, although the Urdu language is also widely spoken.

The cuisine of Andhra Pradesh is reputedly the hottest and spiciest in all of India—and I would agree.

Hyderabad

Hyderabad, the current capital of Andhra Pradesh, was founded in 1591. The city is best known today as the second Silicon Valley of modern India and is fueling the information technology field not only in India and the United States, but also in much of the world. Multinational companies there include Microsoft and Google.

Hyderabad once was the most important foothold of Muslim power in the South. Religiously and culturally, the city is comprised of a large Muslim and Hindu population, who have historically lived there together for over 300 years.

In the nearby hills of Hyderabad were the once-famous Golconda diamond mines. Many famed diamonds, including the Kohinoor and the Hope diamonds, are said to have come from there. Though the mines have now been exhausted and abandoned, until the beginning of the 18th century, India was the sole supplier of diamonds to the world.

The lure of its local diamond industry proved irresistible to the Mughal Emperor Aurangzeb, who captured the region in 1650. One of his generals became the independent ruler of Hyderabad at Aurangzeb's death, and successive Muslim *nizams*, who amassed legendary fortunes, ruled up to the time of India's independence. The 10th and last *nizam,* Mir Osman Ali Khan, came to power in 1911 and was said to be the richest man in the world; his huge palace employed 11,000 servants. When India gained independence in 1947, he refused to relinquish control of the state until Indian troops amassed at his borders forced him to capitulate.

Hyderabad's medieval heritage is still evident through its magnificent mosques, nearby Golconda

Charminar. Hyderabad. 1591.

Fort, and tombs and monuments from the reign of the Qutub Shahi Dynasty. Particularly impressive and known throughout all of India is the Charminar, a gate with four graceful minarets that soar almost 150 feet high. Built over 400 years ago, the Charminar has become the symbol of the city and is considered the legendary masterpiece of the Qutub Shahi legacy. The gate's Indo-Saracenic style is a fitting legacy for the synthesis of the region's Hindu-Muslim traditions.

A few hundred yards from Charminar is the Mekkah Masjid, the oldest mosque in Hyderabad. It is said that the earth to make the bricks used in the construction of its central arch was brought from Mekkah, and hence its name. The largest mosque in southern India, it can accommodate up to 10,000 worshippers at prayer. A room in the courtyard is said to house a relic of the Prophet Mohammed.

Alams. Copies of the standards carried by Imam Hussain in the battle of Karbala, 62 miles southwest of Baghdad, where he was defeated in A.D. 680. Shi'a (Shiite) Muslims consider mourning of that defeat which affected the succession to the Prophet Mohammed to be a sacred event. Hyderabad.

Mekkah Masjid (mosque), Hyderabad. 1614–87.

Tirumala and Tirupathi

Located in the extreme south of Andhra Pradesh, on the top of a holy mountain rising 3,000 feet above the plains, is one of India's most famous Hindu pilgrimage centers, Tirumala, dedicated to Lord Venkateswara, an incarnation of Vishnu. The temple is believed to have existed since ancient times. The mountain's sacredness (Tirumala means holy hill) stems from its many symbolic anecdotes and references in the Hindu *shastras*. In one account, the Lord Himself is said to reside there, having taken the form of a hill. Many deities visited there to worship the Lord, making the cluster of beautiful hills and waterfalls associated with their sojourns sacred.

Tirumala is said to draw more pilgrims annually than either the Vatican or Mekkah (Mecca). It also is one of the richest religious organizations in the world. On any given day, there are usually at least 5,000 pilgrims, though their numbers sometimes swell to 100,000 or more on auspicious occasions! The site owes its popularity to the belief among Hindus that any prayer offered before the statue of Lord Balaji will be granted. Also, many businessmen consider the god to be the patron of commerce.

Pilgrims stand in line for hours to get into the Sri Venkateshwara (Vishnu) Temple, which dates to the 10th century A.D. Some of the more pious devotees make the arduous five-mile, three-hour ascent on foot. For those who wish to reduce their waiting time, purchasing a "special *darshan*" ticket enables the bearer to bypass much of the long queues, where those without a ticket sometimes must wait all day before getting into the temple. It is considered auspicious to have one's hair shaved at Tirumala. As a result, large numbers of men, women, and children may be seen with bald heads.

The organization's immense wealth is put to good use. Its temple trust operates various charities, which support orphanages, hospitals, schools, and universities—not to mention feeding and offering inexpensive accommodations to the vast number of pilgrims who visit Tirumala each day. The temple's staff alone is said to number six thousand.

At the base of the mountain is the sacred town of Tirupathi, which is named after Vishnu. Closely associated with Tirumala, Tirupathi, whose environs include the temple of Lord Venkateswara's consort, Padmavathi Devi, is also an important place of pilgrimage.

A married couple offering their prayers before breaking a coconut, symbolic of surrendering one's ego to God. Tirumala.

Pilgrims observing a priest performing arati *with a flaming lamp. The images of the deities have been removed from the temple and placed in a swing. Tirumala, Andhra Pradesh.*

Women washing clothes near an ancient temple dating from the Chalukyan period. Badami, Karnataka. Mid-6th to mid-8th century.

Vishnu enthroned on the cosmic serpent Ananta. Cave III, Badami. Chalukyan dynasty, ca. A.D. 578.

Karnataka

The juxtaposition of India's ancient heritage with her role as a world leader in modern technology is clearly seen in the state of Karnataka. Though the state is known internationally for its classical Carnatic music, Karnataka's cultural legacy is far broader.

Fifteen hundred years ago, at Badami in the northern part of the state, the Chalukyan dynasty erected some of the oldest-surviving Hindu temples in India, which had considerable influence on South Indian temple architecture. Other important Indian dynasties, such as the Cholas and Gangas, also played their role in Karnataka's history. But it was the exquisite, ornate temples at Belur, Halebid, and Somnathpur, built by the Hoysala dynasty, who ruled between the 11th and 14th centuries, that have prompted some to call Karnataka a marvel of stone architecture. The magnificent archaeological site at Hampi, the temples at Pattadakal, and the elegant Muslim tombs and minarets of Bijapur make this state one of India's less-visited delights.

Bangalore

Bangalore, the capital of Karnataka, is a modern, bustling, cosmopolitan city that attracts people from all over the world. It is the hub of India's science, technology, aircraft, electronics, and computer industries, and is one of the fastest-growing cities in Asia. The city, dubbed the Silicon Valley of India, is home to a large Microsoft center. Although it is an industrial center, Bangalore is, nevertheless, a pleasant city with many parks, gardens, and wide tree-lined avenues.

My fondest memory of the city is my visit to one of its oldest temples, the Bull Temple, which is named after its huge monolithic sculpture of Shiva's Bull, Nandi, which is about 15 feet high and 20 feet long. A little boy standing in front of the altar was too short to see the image of the deity, and kept tugging on his mother's sari until she could ignore him no longer. When she lifted him up for a peek, he leaned over and lovingly kissed the statue. The child's adoration was not unique, and I witnessed similar occurrences at several other shrines.

The Maharaja's Palace. Mysore.

Mysore

Until India's independence, Mysore was the capital city of the maharajas of Mysore, a princely state that covered about a third of the current state of Karnataka. The city has many open areas, which accounts for its being called the "Garden City." Its major architectural attraction is the Indo-Saracenic Maharaja's Palace, with its domes, arches, and colonnades that combine Muslim and Hindu influences. Visitors from all over the world come to see the palace, which was rebuilt in 1912 and contains works of art from many parts of the world.

Man selling strung marigolds to be used as malas *(garlands). Market. Mysore.*

A huge monolithic stone carving of Nandi, the bull associated with Shiva. Chamundi Hills, Mysore. Height: 15 feet. Length: 24 feet.

A palace guard standing in front of a mural.
The Maharaja's Palace. Mysore, Karnataka.

Lord Bahubali (Gomateshvara). Height: 51 feet. Jain. Sravanabelagola. A.D. 981.

Pilgrims. The trident indicates they are devotees of Shiva. Karnataka.

Sravanabelagola

One of the oldest and most important Jain pilgrimage centers is located at Sravanabelagola. The temple is built on top of a hill and is famous for its huge statue of Lord Bahubali (Gomateshvara). The 51-foot-high figure of the Jain saint can be seen from a distance of 15 miles. Carved from a single rock, it is said to be the world's tallest monolithic statue. The word "Sravanabelagola" means "the monk on the top of the hill."

The statue depicts the austere path Bahubali chose to seek enlightenment. Disillusioned with material life, he sought seclusion in a forest and renounced everything—even his clothing. There he stood in rigorous meditation, completely naked, while exposed to the elements. Yet his will never faltered, even though he had no food or sleep. He remained in that posture for so long that anthills grew around him and creepers entwined his limbs. It was only after he shed his ego that he finally attained enlightenment.

In 1981, a special ceremony, which is held every 12 to 14 years, coincided with the 1,000th anniversary of the installation of the statue. As a result, over one million people attended, necessitating the construction of several towns to accommodate the vast number of visitors.

Somnathpur

Some of India's most famous religious monuments are located in Karnataka. They were built during the Hoysala dynasty, which controlled that region from the 11th to 14th centuries. About 25 miles east of Mysore is the Hoysala temple at Somnathpur, built in the second half of the 13th century. The squat, star-shaped temple is one of the more interesting buildings in India. Carved from soapstone (steatite), virtually the entire exterior

Keshava Vishnu Temple. Hoysala dynasty. Somnathpur. A.D. 1268.

of the relatively small temple is covered with superb sculptures. Because soapstone is soft when first quarried, the sculptors were able to carve elaborate details. After a period of exposure to the air, the material hardens and turns dark.

Belur/Halebid

North of Mysore are two temples built during the same period of the Hoysala dynasty. Describing the Hoysala temple at Belur, the 19th century critic, Fergusson, was quoted as saying, "these friezes...carved with a minute elaboration of detail...are one of the most marvelous exhibitions of human labor to be found even in the patient East."[1]

Ten miles from Belur is the Hoysala temple at Halebid, considered by art historians to contain the best examples of Medieval Indian sculpture.

The excursion to the three Hoysala temples and Sravanabelagola was one of the more impressive conducted tours of my entire trip in India, and I would highly recommend it.

A dancing woman. The dance pose is representative of the classical dances of South and East India: Bharata Natyam, Kuchipudi, and Odissi. Keshava Temple, Belur. A.D. 1117.

Mythological animals carved on the pillars of a temple. Hampi.

Golgumbaz, the mausoleum of Mohammed Adil Shah, is said to be the second-largest old dome in the world. Bijapur. 17th century.

Nandi, the bull associated with Shiva. Pattadakal. Height: 8.5 feet.

Gopuram (*gate*). *156 feet high.*
Virupaksha Temple. Hampi,
Karnataka. Mid-15th century.

Kerala

St. Francis Church, Kochi (Cochin). Built by the Portuguese in 1503.

Kerala, one of the smallest states in India, has one of the highest literacy rates in the country. Foreigners have been coming to Kerala for thousands of years, which has given the culture of this state its cosmopolitan blend. The Phoenicians came in search of spices, sandalwood, and ivory. They were followed by the Romans. Later, the Arabs came and dominated spice shipments to Europe. Kerala fishermen still use huge cantilevered fishing nets introduced by the Chinese. Winding streets are lined with Portuguese-style houses, which were built as early as the 15th century.

The state has a unique mixture of religions. Though the majority of Kerala is Hindu, there are also large numbers of Christians and Muslims. Traditional South Indian Kathakali dance-dramas, which date back 500 years, may be seen in the evenings. Their Hindu stories are based on the *Ramayana* and *Mahabharata*.

Christianity had arrived in India 1,400 years before Vasco da Gama sailed around the southern cape of Africa and landed at nearby Kozhikode (Calicut) in 1498. It is said that the Apostle St. Thomas arrived here in A.D. 52, which means Christianity was established in Kerala earlier than in most other places in the world. The earliest Christian communities were Syrian Orthodox, which were there at least as early as A.D. 190. When the Portuguese arrived, they were surprised to find that Christian communities already existed. Because these Christians had never heard of the pope and were not under his authority, the Portuguese tried to suppress their activities. In spite of their efforts, many Syrian Orthodox churches are still active in Kerala today.

It cannot be documented when the first Jews arrived in Kerala, though they probably came with King Solomon's merchant fleet. Some historians believe that the earliest Jews to settle there were descendants of the Jews taken to Babylon by Nebuchadnezzar, and there is ethnomusicological evidence to support that claim. Some scholars think that they once numbered tens of thousands. Their descendants have intermarried with the

Fishing nets. Kovalam Beach.

Cantilevered fishing nets said to be introduced by the Chinese traders from the court of Kublai Khan. Kochi (Cochin).

The courtyard of the synagogue. Kochi (Cochin). 1568.

Hindu population, though their presence still exists. There is still a small community of European Jews, many of whom probably came from Spain after the Spanish Inquisition.

Located on the western seaboard of Kerala is the fishing village of Kovalam. Many say that Kovalam has India's most scenic beaches, and based on the few that I visited, I would agree. A sleepy little hamlet, Kovalam is still unspoiled by the Western culture. The local farmers grow rice, fruits, and vegetables, and life goes on as it always has. I stayed there for four days, enjoying the food and the sun.

Kochi (Cochin)

Kochi (Cochin) is the site of India's oldest European-built church, St. Francis Church, which was constructed by Portuguese Franciscan friars in 1503. Vasco da Gama, who died in Kochi, was buried there for 14 years before his remains were sent to Lisbon, Portugal. His tombstone can still be seen in Kochi.

The Jewish synagogue was built in 1568 and is said to be the oldest in the British Commonwealth. The European Jewish community that has lived around the synagogue since the 16th century once numbered perhaps 4,000, but today, most of them have emigrated to Israel, and only a few families remain. Their emigration to Israel was not motivated by intolerance or discrimination, but by a desire to live in the Jewish state. The Jews were the first large group of foreigners to settle in India and were given a land grant. Because successive Hindu rulers were hospitable to them, India broadened her reputation as a land of tolerance.

It was the Jewish holiday of Passover when I visited the synagogue, and only seven people attended the evening service. The synagogue's floor consisted of 18th-century Chinese blue-and-white porcelain tiles from Guangzhou (Canton), which seemed much too fine to walk upon. Hanging from the ceiling were many crystal chandeliers. The old synagogue is destined to become a museum.

The floor of the synagogue. The porcelain tiles with a blue underglaze were exported from Guangzhou (Canton), China. Kochi (Cochin). 18th century.

Interior of the synagogue.
Kochi (Cochin), Kerala, 1568

Gopuras *(towering entrance gateways) of the Arunachaleshvara Temple complex at the base of the holy mountain of Arunachala.*
Tiruvannamalai.

Tamil Nadu

Many consider Tamil Nadu to have retained the purest essence of ancient Indian culture. Because of its geographical location on the southern tip of the Indian subcontinent, Tamil Nadu remained more isolated than the rest of India from the numerous invaders from the north.

The distinctive landmark of this state is its unique temple architecture. The powerful Dravidian kingdoms erected huge temples over a period of many centuries. The Pallavas, with their capital at Kanchipuram; the Cholas, whose empire flourished from Thanjavur (Tanjore); and the Pandyas, who ruled from Madurai, all left grandiose temple complexes that ensure that their legacies will be long remembered. The ornate temples bear a striking resemblance to each other: the soaring *gopuras* (towering entrance gateways) over all four entrances that were sometimes 13 stories high, the spacious 1000-pillared halls, the long corridors, and the rectangular bathing pools for pilgrims to purify themselves.

Though the people were very polite, it seemed that they were more conservative and less interactive with foreigners than Indians from the north. I was told that religious ritual was an important part of their daily lives. When riding buses in rural areas, I noticed that a man would not take an empty seat next to a woman, even if it meant his having to stand for a long time. Most of the girls and women were immaculately groomed. They dressed in traditional saris, and many wore flowers in their hair, further enhancing their already apparent beauty.

Tiruvannamalai

Rich in tradition and said to be built on a very ancient site, the temple town of Tiruvannamalai is still quite vibrant. The Arunachaleshvara Temple complex, dedicated to Shiva-Parvati, is one of the largest in India. I found the early morning religious activity, combined with ringing of bells and the sonorous chanting of Sanskrit prayers, exhilarating. I could not help but notice how much the giant *gopuras* looked like the Mayan pyramids from the Yucatan Peninsula and Guatemala. I wonder if someday a connection will be made between the art of the two cultures that were oceans apart.

My visit to Tiruvannamalai was made special by my stay at the *ashram* of one of India's great 20th-century saints, Sri Ramana Maharshi. I visited one of the sacred caves on the adjacent holy mountain of Arunachala, where the God-realized sage meditated for many years. Arunachala is considered sacred because Hindus believe the mountain is a manifestation of Shiva, the third aspect of the Hindu Trinity.

Chennai (Madras)

Chennai is the capital of Tamil Nadu and is well-known in the West for its Madras cotton fabrics. Hindu and Islamic architecture, blended with more recent British elements, give many of the municipal buildings an exotic appearance similar to the onion domes of Red Square in Moscow. The museum has an excellent collection of 10th–12th century Chola bronze statuary.

Kanchipuram

Kanchipuram is one of the seven sacred cities for Hindus and served as the capital of three successive kingdoms. The giant *gopuras* (gates) of the spectacular temple complexes can be seen from miles away. Their sight invoked a feeling of awe, and I could imagine that my response had been shared by many of those who had approached the temples, which were over a thousand years old.

Huge temples are located throughout the city. The Pallava, Chola, and Vijayanagar kings who constructed them evidently enjoyed building on a large scale. One of the *gopuras* at a Shiva temple is 192 feet tall. Massive stone walls enclosed a temple complex that is over 22 acres. Inside, there were large rectangular pools of water for purification rites. Some of the temples had halls with a thousand pillars. At a temple dedicated to Vishnu, each of the thousand pillars was artistically carved with that deity riding on a horse.

Dancing Shiva and the elephant-headed Ganesha. Ekambareshwara Temple. Kanchipuram.

Opposite ▷
Vishnu mounted on a horse, Vaikuntaperumal Temple. Kanchipuram. 8th century A.D.

A painted sculpture of a Hindu deity (restored). Airavatesvara Temple. Darasuram. A.D. 1146–63.

A priest of the Airavatesvara Temple. Darasuram.

Pottery horses which serve as guardians of the village. Near Gingee.

A column. Airavatesvara Temple. Darasuram. ca. A.D. 1150.

Mamallapuram (Mahabalipuram)

Mamallapuram (Mahabalipuram) is about 37 miles south of Chennai (Madras). It served as the second capital and seaport of the Pallava dynasty, the first Tamil dynasty of consequence. Among the many important sites to visit is an immense relief carved on the face of a huge rock about 20 feet high and 80 feet long. The carving depicts the descent to earth of the sacred river Ganges through the matted locks of Shiva's hair. It contains over 100 figures of gods, men, and animals.

At the southern edge of Mamallapuram (Mahabalipuram) is a group of five free-standing temples, four of them are carved from the same long granite boulder. They are called *rathas* (chariot), and are "vehicles" to God. Built during the 7th and 8th centuries, they are replicas of ancient wooden structures and are the architectural prototypes of the mammoth South Indian temples which dominate the landscape of Tamil Nadu with their imposing *gopuras*.

Located near the ocean is the Shore Temple, dating to the early 8th century A.D. It is the earliest known example of a stone-built temple in the South. Erected on granite blocks, it has a soaring tower. Its design strongly influenced the architecture of the Cholas, who succeeded the Pallavas as the dominant dynasty in the Tamil region. On the evening I was there, its tiered pyramidal tower made a stunning silhouette against a bright red-orange sunset.

The Descent of the Ganges from Heaven. Mamallapuram (Mahabalipuram). Pallava dynasty, 7th–8th century.

Chidambaram

Chidambaram was a Chola capital from 907 to 1310. I could see the huge temple complex that is dedicated to Shiva as Nataraja, Lord of Dance, from miles away. Two of the huge pyramid-like *gopuras* (entrance gateways) are almost 150 feet high and are carved with the 108 classical postures of Nataraja in his role of cosmic dancer. The complex, which covers over 32 acres, is said to be the oldest in the South. It is considered the Mt. Kailasa (the snow-white Himalayan summit, the mystical abode of Shiva) of South India.

A fire ceremony conducted there in the late afternoon was theatrical. The priest used a large candelabrum to illuminate an image of the dancing Nataraja. The priest's rhythmic arm movements were made more dramatic by the musical accompaniment of a drum and a horn. At moments of intensity, bells were rung.

While wandering through the 1000-pillared hall and admiring the elaborately carved columns, I came upon a small group of students and their Sanskrit teacher sitting on the floor. The scene could have been from ancient times. They were wearing the traditional *dhoti*, which is like a *lungi* or sarong with the cloth pulled up between the legs. Their upper bodies were uncovered. They had religious markings on their foreheads, and their spiritual eyes were marked with a red dot. Their long hair was tied neatly in a knot on the side of their heads, symbolizing the higher state of consciousness that they one day hoped to attain.

The scriptural text, the Vedas, describe the four phases of life in the higher ages of ancient India: *brahmacharya*, a celibate student's life, when one is seeking knowledge; *grahasthya*, a householder's life, when one fulfills worldly responsibilities; *vanaprastha*, a hermit's life, when one withdraws from worldly activities and devotes more time to spirituality; and *sannyasa*, a wanderer or forest dweller's life, when one lives a life of complete renunciation dedicated to seeking Truth.

Young students with their religious teacher. The sacred thread worn over their shoulder indicates they have formally entered adulthood and are to seek higher knowledge. Nataraja Temple. Chidambaram.

The north gopuram (entrance gateway) and the large pool for ritual purification. Nataraja Temple. Chidambaram, Tamil Nadu. 10th century A.D.

◁ *Opposite*
Rajarajeshvara Temple.
Thanjavur (Tanjore).
Chola dynasty, ca. A.D. 1000.

An elephant representing Lord Ganesha, blessing a boy with his trunk. The boy gives a coin to the elephant, who takes it with his trunk and gives it to his keeper. The elephant then blesses the boy on his head, symbolizing Lord Ganesha removing the spiritual obstacles from the boy's life. Rajarajeshvara Temple. Thanjavur (Tanjore).

Thanjavur (Tanjore)

The famous Chola temple in Thanjavur (Tanjore) was built in about A.D. 1000. It is the masterpiece of South Indian architecture. The pyramidal tower rises over the main shrine to a height of 206 feet and is topped with an 81-ton domed capstone, which was raised into place by an earth ramp similar to those used by the Egyptians. The inner courtyard is guarded by one of India's largest Nandis (Shiva's bull), which is carved from a single rock.

In the afternoon, I went to a famous Shiva temple located eight miles away at Thiruvaiyaru. While pilgrims were worshiping at an altar, a priest abruptly closed a curtain, concealing it from view. The priest was symbolically showing us how God plays hide-and-seek with His devotees.

A woman who spoke no English approached me and led me to an obscure shrine, where a priest was performing a fire ritual. As I left the temple, the woman indicated I should follow her. I had no idea what she wanted. We walked for over half a mile, and several times I considered turning back because it was getting dark, and I was ready to return to Thanjavur. We finally reached a small building, and immediately upon entering, I could feel spiritual vibrations pouring into my body. I was puzzled by the experience. A young priest explained to me that this was the shrine of Sri Tyagaraja (1767–1847), a famous saint said to be the greatest musical composer of South India. Aside from being a musical prodigy, he had attained *samadhi*, the highest conscious union with God. Through God's grace, I had been able to feel his vibrations.

Opposite ▷
The west gopuram *(gateway),*
Sri Meenakshi Temple. Madurai.
Nayak dynasty, 17th century.

Our Lady of Good Health Roman
Catholic Church. Velankanni.

Healing Miracles at Velankanni

Pilgrims of all religions flock to a Roman Catholic church in the town of Velankanni because of the many miraculous healings which have taken place there.

The Church of Our Lady of Good Health, located 55 miles southeast of Thanjavur (Tanjore), was dedicated to Mary, Mother of Jesus, by a group of Portuguese sailors. Their boat was about to capsize in a violent storm when she appeared and saved them from drowning. Another sighting of Mary occurred close by, and a shrine now marks that location.

The large chapel dedicated to Mary was filled with devotees of various faiths who were praying there. Some Indians, probably Hindus, removed their shoes in the church, others did not. The ecumenical gathering foreshadowing the peace yet possible in today's world, inspired me.

The object of veneration was a statue of Mary holding the baby Jesus. Both Mary and the Christ child were wrapped in orange cloth which only exposed their faces. Each wore a regal red crown, richly ornamented with gold. A variety of jeweled ornaments hanging from the image of Mary looked like fetishes. The effigy could have been equally at home in any religion which uses icons.

A museum to honor the numerous healings which had taken place was located next door to the church. Glass cases displayed letters attesting to the particular healing which occurred. Many had enclosed gold or silver replicas of the cured body parts. Some sent jewelry or other offerings.

I, too, received a physical healing at Velankanni. For the previous two weeks, I had been having terrible stomach pains every time I ate, and I was deeply concerned about my condition. After leaving the museum, I noticed that I had no ill effects when I ate the food I purchased for my two-hour bus ride back to Thanjavur. From that day to this, I have never again had stomach pains. Thinking back to that morning in Velankanni, I remember the exact moment when God responded to my tearful prayer.

Madurai

The famous Sri Meenakshi Temple attracts thousands of visitors a day. The temple covers about 15 acres in the middle of the city and draws pilgrims from all over India. Its enormous 150-foot-high, nine-story-tall gate is covered with brightly painted gods, goddesses, and animals.

One afternoon, I went to the Gandhi Museum. Because of my reverence for "the Father of Modern India," I visited as many sites associated with Gandhi as possible. The museum displayed his blood-stained *dhoti*, which he was wearing on the day that he was assassinated. When the great man fell dying to the ground, his last earthly act was to raise his hand in a peaceful gesture, blessing his assailant.

Rameswaram

En route to the southern tip of India, I visited Rameswaram, located on an island in the Gulf of Mannar. The town has one of the most important temples in the South, which is a fine example of Dravidian architecture. Begun in the 12th century A.D., additions were made over succeeding centuries. Its magnificent corridors are lined with finely-carved pillars. One of the corridors is 4,000 feet long and is the longest in India.

Kanyakumari, Tamil Nadu

Kanyakumari: Where Three Oceans Meet

Kanyakumari is the southernmost point of India and is where the Bay of Bengal, the Indian Ocean, and the Arabian Sea merge. It was here that I visited a special Gandhi Memorial. A portion of the great saint's ashes had been enshrined on a pedestal prior to being placed in the ocean there. Peaceful emanations marked the spot where his ashes once sat. Such is the legacy of those who have known peace.

Built on two rocky islands 200 yards offshore on an island is the Vivekananda Memorial. The imposing beauty of the temple is enhanced by its natural setting. Built in 1970, the temple incorporates architectural styles from all over India. At the base of the dark rocky island, white waves broke gently upon massive boulders. As the afternoon sun set on the temple's stone surface, its central dome and upper portions glowed soft mauve.

The temple honors Swami Vivekananda, who went there in 1892 to meditate before leaving for the West to share the wisdom of Hinduism. The foremost disciple of the great Indian sage Sri Ramakrishna, Swami Vivekananda was invited to attend the World Parliament of Religions in Chicago in September 1893.

The swami received an overwhelming response from the audience of 7,000 and brought them to their feet when he said:

> Sisters and Brothers of America, it fills my heart with joy unspeakable to rise in response to the warm and cordial welcome which you have given us. I thank you in the name of the most ancient order of monks in the world, I thank you in the name of the mother of all religions, and I thank you in the name of the millions and millions of Hindu people of all classes and sects. I am proud to belong to a religion which has brought the world both tolerance and universal acceptance. We believe not only in universal tolerance, but we accept all religions to be true.

Vivekananda Memorial. Kanyakumari. 1970.

Shiva as Nataraja (Lord of Dance). Bronze. Art Gallery. Thanjavur (Tanjore). Chola dynasty, 11th–12th century.

In Hinduism, Shiva as an instrument of Cosmic Intelligence brings all things into physical creation and dissolves all things back into the One. In his upper right hand he holds a *damaru*, a hand drum, that made the first sound of creation. In his upper left hand he holds the *agni*, the fire, that will dissolve the universe back into the One, Unmanifested Spirit. The dwarflike figure trampled by his right foot represents illusion (*maya* or Satan), which leads humankind astray. The iconography is identical to the words of Christ: "I am alpha and omega, the beginning and the end, the first and the last" (Revelation 22:13).

Epilogue

The German philosopher Goethe said that to live in another's country and to speak another's language increases one's knowledge tenfold. I certainly would agree. Our shrinking world makes it easier today than ever before to adopt the best from all civilizations. Certainly no nation or religion has a monopoly on truth. West and East have much to share.

Of all of the nations in the world, India is the most spiritually blessed. More and more Americans are learning that materialism does not give lasting satisfaction, and they are turning to India for spiritual guidance.

The most sublime purpose of religion is to teach us how to know God. Once we become aware of the spark of God within us (the soul), we realize that we are all interconnected children of the Most High. Then we understand that there is but one religion with many denominations. All religions lead to God, and it does not matter which path one follows, for the multicolored lamps of each faith burn with the same white flame.

I do not suggest that the various forms of religious worship be made homogeneous, for each appeals to the particular culture to which it was brought. Rituals and symbols may vary, but the principles they represent are universal. Once we experience the God within, religious prejudice disappears.

I believe that religion should offer a scientific basis by which the practitioner may know God. Yoga meditation is the scientific way to experience God-communion. By consciously withdrawing the mind from the restless senses, one's attention can be placed upon God. Meditation makes God knowable to ordinary people through the framework of their existing religion. The Bible says: "Be still, and know that I am God" (Psalms 46:10). Once the mind becomes calm, the image of the Divine is reflected within.

When Albert Einstein said, "Science without religion is lame, and religion without science is blind," he could have been describing contemporary America and India. India has become overbalanced spiritually and cannot adequately provide for the material needs of its own people. America leads the world in consumer comforts, but has veered sharply off course morally. Each culture would benefit from adopting the best qualities of the other. It is my belief that the United States and India can give the world a new direction: a materially efficient democracy that is spiritually guided. For this to become a reality, each of us must do our part. By changing ourselves, we will change the world.

Chapter Notes

Dedication
1. Paramahansa Yogananda, *Songs of the Soul*, (Los Angeles: Self-Realization Fellowship, 1983), 171.

Introduction
1. Paramahansa Yogananda, "Thou hast many Names," *Whispers from Eternity* (Los Angeles: Self-Realization Fellowship, 1959), 143.

Chapter Two: The East
1. Located in downtown Kolkata (Calcutta), the temple is believed to be about 200 years old. It also is known as Kalighat and should not be confused with the Kali Temple associated with Sri Ramakrishna, located in the suburb of Dakshineswar.

2. The 6th century B.C. saw the birth of many extraordinary spiritual and philosophical geniuses: Confucius and Lao-tzu in China, Pythagoras and Heraclitus in Greece, the Hebrew prophet Zechariah, the Jain prophet Mahavira, and the Hindu Upanishadic sages in India.

Chapter Three: The North
1. Sri Daya Mata, "The Inner Paradise of Even-Mindedness," *Self-Realization* (Los Angeles: Self-Realization Fellowship, Spring, 1991), 10–2.

2. Paramahansa Yogananda, *Autobiography of a Yogi* (Los Angeles: Self-Realization Fellowship, 1985), 389.

3. Sri Gyanamata, *God Alone* (Los Angeles: Self-Realization Fellowship, 1984), 26.

4. The following story has been summarized from Ananda K. Coomaraswamy and Sister Nivedita, *Myths of Hindus and Buddhists* (New York: Dover Publications, 1967), 369–70.

Chapter Five: The West
1. The spiritually advanced yogi probably had attuned his consciousness with God and could heal others in accordance with the Divine Will. What herb or medicine he gave to them is of no importance, but it probably served to awaken their greater faith.

Chapter Six: The South
1. James Fergusson, *A History of Indian and Eastern Architecture*, Vol. I (New Delhi, 1967), 448.

Glossary*

Aryans (Sanskrit). A term incorrectly ascribed to a group of people who supposedly invaded India from Central Asia in the second millenium B.C. This theory of invasion originated from British scholarship based on limited excavations conducted from the late 19th to the early 20th century. Modern scholarship, however, has shown that the highly advanced culture that developed along the Indus River was the product of indigenous peoples already living in the region. In that context, what is known as the Indus River civilization today should in fact be called the Sindu-Saraswati River civilization which was mentioned in the ancient Hindu scriptures, the Vedas. Satellite imaging, supported by limited excavations, has revealed the course of the ancient Saraswati River.

The ancient Sanskrit word "Aryan" means one who is noble and spiritually advanced. It was also used as a title of respect for kings and had no racial connotation whatsoever. The culture of the Aryans was based upon the belief that the whole world is one family.

ashram. A spiritual residence. The Hindu equivalent of a monastery or hermitage.

Aum (Om). The basis of all sounds. *Aum* of the Hindu Vedas became the sacred word *Hum* to the Tibetans; *Amin* to the Moslems; and *Amen* of the Egyptians, Greeks, Romans, Jews, and Christians. *Aum* is the all-pervading sound emanating from the Holy Ghost; the Word of the Bible; the voice of creation testifying to the Divine Presence in every atom.

avatar. A soul who has attained union with Spirit, and then returned to earth to help humankind; a divine incarnation.

Bhakti Yoga (devotion). The path to God which emphasizes all-surrendering love and adoration as the principal means for communion and union with God.

Bodhisattva. In Buddhism, one who has almost attained the state of *nirvana* (liberation), but who renounces it and retains his human form on earth to help others.

darshan (holy sight). A special blessing received from seeing a holy person. Visiting a holy site where a saint has been, or where sacred relics are contained, is also considered *darshan*.

dharma. The eternal principles of righteousness that upholds all creation; humankind's inherent duty to live in harmony with these principles.

dhoti. A male garment knotted around the waist, similar to a *lungi* (sarong), but the cloth is pulled up between the legs.

Dravidian. A term applied today to the peoples and languages of four modern states of South India. These states are Tamil Nadu, Kerala, Andhra Pradesh and Karnataka. References to these regions occur in the ancient Hindu literature such as the *Mahabharata*. These peoples have greatly enriched the literature, the arts, and culture of India.

India had many principalities in the past, and their names have changed many times. The major language of the principality of Dravid was ancient Tamil. Calling the Tamil language Dravidian is a linguistic distinction of the 19th century.

In India, people were (and still are) referred to by the region's name. The fact that the people were called Dravidian would seem to indicate that they were native to that area. There is no evidence that they were forced there from somewhere else.

ghat. Long rows of steps leading down to a river which facilitate devotees getting to the water.

guru (spiritual teacher). When devotees are earnest in their search for God, the Lord sends them a guru. A guru is much more than just an ordinary teacher. He is a living manifestation of scriptural truths and is able to guide and direct

*Many of the metaphysical definitions are based on glossaries in Self-Realization Fellowship's books by Paramahansa Yogananda, such as Man's Eternal Quest *and* Where There Is Light.

Glossary

his disciples to final realization. Without a guru, an ordinary person will never attain Self-realization. Today in the West, the word guru has been corrupted to mean "a teacher with a large following."

Jnana Yoga (wisdom). The path to union with God by transforming the discriminative power of the intellect into the all-knowing wisdom of the soul.

karma (effects of past action). The law of *karma* is the effect of an individual's past actions, which may be from this life or previous lifetimes. Every religion in the world teaches a similar concept of action and reaction, cause and effect, or sowing and reaping.

Any action a person commits, whether it be good or bad, sets in motion a similar pattern of occurrences that will inexorably return like a boomerang to the doer in the present or a future existence. Thus, each person becomes the creator of his or her own destiny. What the Western mind views as fate would be looked upon by the Hindu as a moral consequence. Once one understands that *karma* is the universe's law of justice, an individual accepts responsibility for his or her circumstances and no longer harbors resentments against God or people.

The collective actions of people within communities, countries, or the world create "mass *karma*," which produces local or global consequences depending on the preponderance of the good or evil committed. The thoughts and actions of every person, therefore, are important and contribute to maintaining the well-being of the world.

Karma Yoga (service). The path to union with God through selfless service, performing all work and actions with an attitude of non-attachment. By seeing God as the sole Doer and giving the results of one's actions to Him, an individual may become freed from the bondage of the ego.

Krishna. The eighth incarnation of Vishnu whose picture is often blue, the color of infinity. Krishna is the most popular Hindu deity whose counsel to his disciple Arjuna is given in the most beloved Hindu scripture the Bhagavad Gita. The central message of the Gita is that men and women may attain liberation through love for God, wisdom, and performance of right actions in the spirit of non-attachment.

linga. A phallic shrine object, usually carved of stone, which represents Shiva's (the third aspect of the Hindu Trinity) creative role within the universe.

mahasamadhi. The last meditation or conscious communion with God, known beforehand to a perfected master, when he merges himself in the Holy Spirit or cosmic sound of *Aum* or Amen as he gives up his physical body. From the Sanskrit *maha* which means great, and *samadhi* which means state of God-union.

mantra. Sacred root word sounds which have a spiritually beneficial vibratory effect upon the person who repeats them.

master. One who has attained self-mastery, as evidenced by his ability to enter at will the breathless state of *sabikalpa samadhi* or the higher state of immutable bliss of *nirbikalpa samadhi*.

Mughal (also spelled Moghul). The Muslim dynasty of Indian emperors. The six greatest Moghul emperors were Babur, Humayun, Akbar, Jahangir, Shah Jahan, and Aurangzeb. These six ruled from 1527 to 1707, though the dynasty continued until 1858.

pranam. A ritual gesture of respect performed by placing the fingers and palms of both hands together and slightly bowing the head.

pranayama. The conscious control of *prana* (life energy), or currents of subtle energy flow in the body which activate and sustain life.

prasad. Food (sweets, fruit, etc.) offered to a deity or a living saint, which is sanctified because it has been blessed. It is distributed by priests in the temples and may be eaten there or taken away to share with others.

Glossary

Raja Yoga (the royal road). The path to union with God considered by Krishna in the Bhagavad Gita to be the highest path. Raja Yoga incorporates the most effective methods from the other yoga paths, and teaches that scientific meditation is the basis for God-realization. *Raja Yoga* leads to perfect development of the body, mind, and soul.

reincarnation. A doctrine which states that human beings who die with unfulfilled material desires have to return to earth again and again, until they are able to reclaim their divine status as children of God. "Him that overcometh will I make a pillar in the temple of my God, and he shall go no more out" (Revelation 3:12).

The early Christian Church accepted the principle of reincarnation, which was expounded by the Gnostics and by numerous Church fathers, including Clement of Alexandria, Origen, and St. Jerome. The doctrine was first declared a heresy in A.D. 553 by the Second Council of Constantinople.

sadhu. An anchorite; one devoted to asceticism and spiritual discipline.

Sanskrit. The oldest surviving language and the most perfect phonetic language in use. It is grouped in the Indo-European family of languages. The language of the Vedas originated in India. Sanskrit has influenced many languages of modern Europe.

spiritual eye. Located at the point between the eyebrows. It is where meditators concentrate their attention when meditating. The spiritual eye is the entryway through which a yogi or a yogini passes his or her consciousness into the higher realms, and experiences the Father, Son, and Holy Ghost. Jesus spoke of the divine light that is perceived through the spiritual eye when He said: "When thine eye is single [if the two physical eyes focus into the one spiritual eye], thy whole body also is full of light....Take heed therefore that the light which is in thee be not darkness" (Luke 11:34-35). Hindu women mark the spiritual eye on their foreheads with a red spot which is known as a *bindi* or *tilak*. The spiritual eye usually is portrayed on the images of saints.

Sri. A title of respect which means holy or revered when used before the name of a religious person. In the South, the anglicized spelling becomes Shree and in West India, it is spelled Shri.

Sufism. The mystical teachings of Islam whose forms vary across the Islamic world.

swami. A monk who is a member of Hinduism's most ancient monastic order, which was reorganized by Swami Shankara in the ninth century. A swami takes formal vows of poverty (renunciation of worldly possessions and ambitions), celibacy, and obedience to spiritual authority. He follows the path of meditation and other spiritual practices, and dedicates himself to service to humanity. The Sanskrit word swami means "he who is one with the Self (*Swa*)."

Trinity (the threefold nature of Spirit when it manifests creation). The theologies of all major religions agree with the ancient Hindu interpretation that when Spirit manifests creation, It becomes the Trinity: *Sat, Tat, Aum*, or the Father, Son, Holy Ghost. *Sat*, (the Father), in the impersonal sense, is God as the Creator without form existing beyond creation *Tat* (the Son), is God's omnipresent intelligence reflecting in an undisturbed state throughout creation. *Aum* (the Holy Ghost) is the active vibratory creative power of God that objectifies or structures creation.

In Hinduism, the impersonal aspect of God the Father as Creator becomes Brahma, who resides beyond the physical universe of space, time, and matter. Vishnu represents the Son, who is the Sustainer or Preserver of the universe; and Shiva personifies the third part of the Hindu Trinity, the Holy Ghost who manifests, destroys or dissolves all things back into the One, Unmanifested Spirit.

Yoga. One of the six systems of the Hindu philosophy. A technique of spiritual and physical training by which an individual soul may be united with the Unmanifested Spirit.

yogi. A male practitioner of Yoga.

yogini. A female practitioner of Yoga.

Index

Index

Index

Lothal, ancient port of Gujarat, 151, 168
lotus, symbol of the expansion of the soul, 30
Lourdes, France, Christian pilgrimage site, 47
lungi*, cloth worn like a sarong by males, 147

M

Madras (see Chennai)
Madurai, city in Tamil Nadu, site of famous temple, 179, 204–05
Mahabalipuram (see Mamallapuram)
Mahabharata, ancient epic, 8, 81, 137, 170, 192
Mahavira, 132, 209
Mahabodhi Temple, site of the Buddha's enlightenment, Bodh Gaya, 69–70, 72
Mahalakshmi temple, Bombay, 154–55
Mahayana Buddhism, majority sect spreading to China, Korea, and Japan, 157
Mamallapuram (Mahabalipuram), Tamil Nadu, ancient monuments, 176–77, 179
mani stones, Buddhist, Ladakh, 123
mantra*, potent chant, 211
marriage, arranged, 172–75
master*, Self-realized soul, 1, 11, 92, 211
Mathura, Uttar Pradesh, birthplace of Krishna, 86
Mauryan Empire, first true empire of India, 29
Mecca (see Mekkah)
Mekkah, 27, 142, 181
Modhera, Gujarat, site of ancient sun temple, 151, 162
Mohammed, prophet and founder of Islam religion, 9, 181
Mohammed Ghaus, 16th century Sufi saint, tomb in Gwalior, 38
Mohenje-daro, ancient city of Indus Civilization, 168
monsoon, 55
mosques, 26–7, 81, 85–6, 95, 162–63, 181
Moti Masjid (Pearl Mosque), Agra, 85
Mother Teresa of Calcutta, 44, 54, 155
Mountbatten, Lord, last British Viceroy, 83
Mt. Abu, hill station in Rajasthan, site of Jain Dilwara Temples, 127, 146–47, 165
Mt. Kanchenjunga, world's third highest mountain, 56–7, 63
Mt. Kailasa, mystical Himalayan abode of Shiva, 200
mudra, ritual position of hands and fingers, 96
Mughal*, Muslim Dynasty of Indian emperors, 2, 23, 26, 84, 110, 112, 115, 127, 129, 180, 211
Mumbai (Bombay), seaport and capital of Maharashtra, 2, 10, 30, 81, 151, 154–55, 169
Muslims, 7, 9 26–7, 38, 44, 79–80, 84, 86, 110, 141–42, 163, 179–81, 185–86, 192
Mysore, city in Karnataka, 179, 186–89

N

Nalanda, site of ancient Buddhist university in Bihar, 43, 74
Nandi, Shiva's bull, 185–86, 190
Nataraja, Shiva in his role of Cosmic Dancer, 196, 200–01, 207
Narmada River, 5, 35
Nebuchadnezzar, King of Babylonia and conqueror of Jerusalem, 192
Nehru, Jawaharlal, India's first Prime Minister, 83
New Delhi, capital of India, 69, 79, 81–4
nirvana, Buddhism, extinction of dualistic existence, 29, 37, 71–3, 96, 210

non-attachment, principle taught by Krishna in Bhagavad Gita, 11, 86, 88, 211
Notovitch, Nicholas, Russian traveler to Ladakh, 120

O

Old Delhi, capital of Muslim India, 81, 83, 85
Old Goa, village in Goa, location of Portuguese cathedrals, 152–53
Omkareshwar, town in Madhya Pradesh, 5, 15, 34–8
Orchha, capital of 17th century Rajput kingdom, Madhya Pradesh, iv–v, 15, 22–4

P

Palitana, site of Jain holy mountain in Gujarat, 151, 164-65
Pallava Dynasty, South India, 180, 195–96, 199
Panaji, state capital of Goa, 148–49, 151, 153
palaces, 23–4, 124–25, 128–31, 136, 186–87
Panjim (see Panaji)
Parsis, followers of teachings of Zarathustra, 7, 154
Parvati, an aspect of God as Divine Mother, consort of Shiva, 195
Patan, step well, Gujarat, 150
Pattadakal, town in Karnataka, 190
Pelling, town in Sikkim, 63
Pharisees, ancient sect of Jews, 120
Pilate, Pontius, Roman governor of Judea when Christ was crucified, 120
Polo, Marco, Venetian traveler to India, quoted, 108
Portuguese, 151–54, 192–93
Poussin, Nicolas, 17th century French classical painter, 37
Puranas, ancient Hindu sacred texts, 108, 182
Puri, holy city in the state of Orissa, 37, 43, 64, 67, 120
Pushkar, city in Rajasthan, 127, 138–40
prana, universal creative energy, life force, 49
pranam*, ritual gesture of respect, 155
pranayama*, yoga technique for control of life force, 48
prasad*, Divinely blessed sweets, 30, 49, 139, 211

Q

Qur'an (Koran), Holy book of Islam, 9, 26, 163
Qutub Minar, Delhi, 82-3
Qutub Shahi Dynasty, 180–81

R

Raja Yoga, royal or complete yogic path, 71, 212
Rajgir, city in Bihar, 74–5
Rajputs, warrior clans who controlled Rajasthan, 23, 127, 129, 134
Ramadan, ninth month of the Mohammedan year, daily fast from dawn until sunset, 27, 141
Ramakrishna, Paramahansa, a yogic master, guru of Vivekananda, 47, 92, 206, 209
Ramana Maharshi, a God-realized sage, 195
Ramayana, ancient Hindu epic, 8, 192
Rameswaram, important Hindu pilgrimage temple located on island in Gulf of Mannar, Tamil Nadu, 3, 179, 206
Ranakpur, Rajasthan, location of largest Jain temple, 127, 132–33
Ranchi, city in Jharkhand, 43
reincarnation *, 8, 9, 212
religions, in India, 8–9
Rig Veda, earliest of Sanskrit scriptures of India and chief of the four Vedas, 8

Index